Babe Ruth: The Inspiring Story of One of Baseball's Greatest Legends

An Unauthorized Biography

By: Clayton Geoffreys

Visit my website at www.claytongeoffreys.com
Cover photo by Irwin, La Broad, & Pudlin is licensed under CC0 / modified from original

Table of Contents

Foreword

If you were to ask anyone on the street to name a famous baseball player, it wouldn't take long before Babe Ruth's name would be mentioned. Babe Ruth, also known as "The Bambino", is one of the most renowned American sports icons of all time, and also one of the greatest if not the greatest baseball player of all time. Ruth won seven World Series Championships, and was the American League's home run leader twelve different times. It is pretty easy to say that Ruth dominated the game of baseball throughout his career. Thank you for purchasing *Babe Ruth: The Inspiring Story of One of Baseball's Greatest Legends.* In this unauthorized biography, we will learn Babe Ruth's incredible life story and impact on the game of baseball. Hope you enjoy and if you do, please do not forget to leave a review!

Also, check out my website at claytongeoffreys.com to join my exclusive list where I let you know about my latest books. To thank you for your purchase, you can go to my site to download a free copy of *33 Life Lessons: Success Principles, Career Advice & Habits of Successful People*. In the book, you'll learn from some of the greatest thought leaders of different industries on what it takes to become successful and how to live a great life. I'll also gift you a few more of my sports biographies.

Cheers,

Clayton Geoffreys

Visit me at www.claytongeoffreys.com

Introduction

The Sultan of Swat. The Big Fellow. The Colossus of Clout. Jidge. The Big Bam. The Behemoth of Bust. The Maharajah of Mash. The Mammoth of Maul. The King of Swing. The Great Bambino. Or as you know him best, The Babe.

When we talk about the greatest athletes to ever play a sport, names that come to mind include Tom Brady, Michael Jordan, Wayne Gretzky, Roger Federer, Tiger Woods, Jack Nicklaus, Muhammad Ali, Jim Brown, and Michael Phelps. These are all guys from our generation or maybe the generation before. They are still fresh in the minds of most people.

But atop the list for many is George Herman Ruth, simply known as The Babe, as in Babe Ruth. For a man to have his legend stay intact for so long, over 100 years since he started playing the game of baseball, says volumes about the former Red Sox and Yankees slugger.

We talk about legacy in sports and wanting to leave behind the best one possible. There may be no greater legacy in sports than the one Babe Ruth established for others to emulate and remember. When people talk about the home run king, they do not mention recent stars like Barry Bonds, Mark McGwire, or Alex Rodriguez. It is usually Babe Ruth. Before the iconic Yankees Stadium was torn down in 2008, it was known as "The House that Ruth Built." When you walk into Monument Park, the first thing you see is Babe Ruth.

Not many people can say that they actually remember Ruth as a living person. After all, he began playing in 1914 and retired in 1935. But the stories of Ruth have been carried on for generations and the respect that others have gathered for him has only gotten stronger with time. He is more than a hero and more than a legend now. He has become a transcendental icon who represents everything we love and esteem about baseball itself.

Ruth's story is definitely worthy of that admiration. It has many memorable moments from beginning to end, with a long list of ups and downs. His was one of the most interesting and exciting lives that anyone could ever experience. He had it all—and the larger-than-life personality to go with it.

While we may know Babe Ruth the athlete, there was also Babe Ruth the person. Was he perfect? No, definitely not. He had a temper and his behavior was a bit unorthodox at times. Some have speculated that he was not the most faithful husband early on in his life and that he sometimes deliberately picked fights with others. In other words, in many ways, he was much like every other athlete, simply a man as flawed as the rest of us, but living his life in the public eye and not behind closed doors. What set him apart the most, though, was the good side of him. He cared for others, was as generous an athlete as there ever was, and did a lot for the youth of America. In fact, he was known as the "Boss of the Youth of America."[iv]

Ruth often visited children in hospitals who were struggling to liven up their spirits. He would spend time talking baseball with young kids and teaching them about the game. He would hand out baseballs to children at games or hit home runs for them to give them something to be happy about. He had a connection with the younger generation that perhaps no other athlete in history has ever had. It was not for show, either; bear in mind that the media of 1920 was not exactly the media of 2020. You did not really do things for show back then, or for the cameras. There was no television. He was generous and kind because of the huge heart that he had. There are countless stories that will be shared here and countless more that will not be mentioned of how Ruth inspired the children of America and helped shape the game of baseball for future generations to come. Who knows if the younger generation in the 1920s would have grown to love the game and pass it on to their children if Babe Ruth did not exist? If not for Ruth, baseball might not even be America's favorite pastime as it is today.

As a player, Ruth was the best. There is no denying that. He was both a pitcher and a hitter. He started with the Red Sox before being traded to the Yankees in what was dubbed the "Sale of the Century," which launched the beginning of the infamous Red Sox curse that lasted nearly 100 years (during which the hapless Sox could not win a World Series). In his 22 years as a player, Ruth hit .342 with a slugging average of .690, the highest of anyone in history. He finished with 714 home runs, including four seasons where he had 54 or more of them. Ruth won seven World Series championships, helping lead the Red Sox to three and the Yankees to four. He hit an incredible .326 in 10 World Series appearances with a slugging percentage of .744.[i]

Ruth's best season came perhaps in 1923, a season in which he hit .393 with 41 home runs and 130 runs batted in. That season he was awarded the MVP for Major League Baseball. Ruth stands 2nd and 3rd all-time for highest slugging percentage in a season as well, hitting .846 and .847 in back-to-back seasons in 1920 and 1921. He led the league in home runs 12 times, led in RBIs 5 times, led in runs scored 8 times, led in walks 11 times, and led in slugging percentage 13 times.

Unlike some of the home run leaders today, there was no speculation of Babe Ruth ever doing anything illegal in how he hit the ball. In fact, there is a common saying out there that while guys like Bonds, McGwire, and Sosa did it (hit home runs) on steroids, Babe Ruth did it on hot dogs and beer. Perhaps that is true. Ruth was not exactly the most built ballplayer for much of his career. He did not have the muscle mass of a Pujols or a Trout, nor did he have the slim body of a Jeter or an Ichiro. He was a bit in-between. His health and weight were never really a priority in his life. Hitting the baseball was, and he was darn good at it.

Babe Ruth inspired love of the game during a dark time in baseball and in America. Early in his career, he made people forget about the Black Sox scandal of 1919, in which members of the Chicago White Sox deliberately threw the World Series in a gambling fix. Later in his career, the nation was struggling through The Great Depression and baseball seemed to take a backseat to the crisis that was overwhelming the country and its citizens. But Ruth used the opportunity to entertain fans and get their minds off their problems. People stopped what they were doing and forgot about their financial worries just to watch The Babe.

In 1936, Ruth was one of the first five players ever inducted into the Hall of Fame. His lifelong dream was to become an MLB manager one day, but he never achieved it. Many clubs worried about his sometimes-flamboyant lifestyle and the fact that his persona did not always evince conservative family values. While he was known as one of the most generous men alive, regularly giving to charities, he also had the reputation of having a nightlife consumed with alcohol and women. While it subsided as he grew older and Ruth had mostly settled down by the time he retired, that history still made ball clubs nervous about hiring him. He did coach the Brooklyn Dodgers as an assistant in 1938 before being asked to leave. Every time it seemed like he would get close to being a manager, a feud erupted that hurt his chances.

Ruth also battled illness towards the middle and end of his career and it got worse with time. While early hospitalizations were regarded as just cases of cold and flu, it became something much more and his declining health was showing in his final years as a player. In 1942, Ruth suffered his worst illness when he was diagnosed with pneumonia. Then in 1946, Ruth was experiencing extreme pain in his left eye and was getting severe migraines. Doctors found a cancerous tumor in his neck that required an operation.

The surgery was somewhat successful, but some of the tumor still lingered in his throat. Ruth remained very ill and lost a considerable amount of weight. He still made a rare public appearance, however. He visited Yankees Stadium in 1947 on "Babe Ruth Day" and told the fans there, "The only real game in the world, I think, is baseball. v

In 1948, Ruth made his final appearance at Yankees Stadium and received an incredible ovation from the crowd, unlike any other. His health was very poor by that point and, shortly after the event, he went back into the hospital and sadly, never left. Ruth passed away on Aug. 16, 1948, from throat cancer. While his body may have died, his spirit would live on forever and the memories he created for the entire world would never be forgotten.

What Babe Ruth did for baseball was nothing short of miraculous. He helped bring the game to life, a game that would most certainly not be the same today if not for him. His unique style and swagger made the game interesting and fun. His extraordinary talent made the game exciting. His enduring love for baseball and for the people around him made him a role model that all young athletes wanted to emulate.

Nowadays, any time someone mentions the name "Babe," the first thing someone thinks of is the baseball player that helped make the game what it is. Babe Ruth was the King of Baseball. Many would probably say he still is.

Chapter 1: Early Childhood

Born George Herman Ruth on February 6, 1895, it took just 19 years for Ruth to acquire the name "Babe" rather than being called George. Much of how he got that name was because he really had no parents around growing up (more on this later on). Ruth was born in Baltimore in 1895 to George and Kate and was one of eight children in the family, although only he and his sister, Mamie, survived to reach adulthood.[v]

George very rarely got to see his parents because they were always working. The late 1800s and early 1900s were a grinding time for adults trying to make ends meet, particularly George's parents, who came from German and Irish descent. Both George, Sr. and Kate worked at a bar with George, Sr. being a bartender. They worked nearly every day from morning until close to make a living. Because of that, George, Jr. barely saw his mother and father.

Making matters more difficult for George, Sr. and Kate was that George, Jr. was not a well-behaved child. He often got himself into trouble around Baltimore, mostly with workers around the docks. He picked fistfights with other kids and even adults, threw tomatoes at police officers, chewed tobacco, and even drank alcohol at just seven years old. He lacked guidance and discipline, mostly because he had no supervision. His parents were simply never around, and when they were, they did not know how to handle him.[v]

It is not uncommon. Some kids who grow up poor and in a difficult environment struggle early in life, and when you do not have anyone to truly take care of you, you misbehave. You do not know any better at that age. It happened years ago and it still happens today. George, Jr., unfortunately, was a victim of being forgotten and not having people to teach him right from wrong.

Another reason for George's erratic and hyperactive behavior was that he suffered from ADHD (Attention Deficit Disorder). It was not diagnosed at the time but was found out later on in his life. It also played a major role in his baseball career when he was older in a positive way, much like it helped Albert Einstein, Thomas Edison, and Mozart, all of whom also had it.[v]

Instead of disciplining their son and showing him right from wrong, George's parents sent him away. They did not feel like they had the time to work with their son or the patience to deal with him, so they sent him to St. Mary's Industrial School for Boys in Baltimore. The school was for discipline, to help mend troubled boys. George begged to return home, crying every day and pleading to let him go back to his parents, but his parents said no and the school kept him.

It was not an easy school. It would be a difficult experience early on that would further influence George later in life. The school was run by The

Brothers of the Order of St. Francis Xavier and supervised boys who had no families, had been given away by their parents, and had juvenile court offenses.[vi]

George's everyday routine was not exactly fun. He would wake up at 6:00 a.m., wash and dress for mass and breakfast…then classes—academic or vocational—from breakfast until 10 in the morning. Recess from 10 to 10:30 a.m. School or work from 10:30 to 11:30 a.m. Dinner and free time 11:30 to 1:30 p.m. School again until 3:15 p.m., after which time there was a class in Catholic doctrine, required of Catholics only. From then until supper at 6:00 p.m. the boys played, the small boys in the Little Yard, and the boys of fifteen or older in the Big Yard. After supper, the boys read in bed from 7:30 p.m. until lights out 45 minutes later.[vi]

Imagine that strict and regimental experience, especially for a hyperactive child who was heretofore unsupervised. It was like that every single day. But while it was not easy, it helped improve George's behavior. In his free time, he also learned a new favorite pastime that would help shape his life forever—baseball!

Learning the Game

While Ruth spent his time going to classes, working, and making shirts as his trade, during his free time he played baseball, as was customary for boys at St. Mary's. Seven different sports were played there, but baseball was most boys' sport of choice. It was positively revered there. There were even tournaments between different dormitories. Because of his larger-than-average size, 8-year-old George was playing with 12-year-olds. When he was 12, he was playing with 16-year-olds. When he was 16, he was on the varsity team playing with guys who were 20. And while he was big in size, he was not overweight. George was actually thin and muscular at that time in his life, contrary to what others say. He would not get heavier until later in his life.[vi]

George was good at baseball from the start. Very good, in fact. He even surprised himself at how well he could hit the ball. Brother Mathias, a school disciplinarian at St. Mary's, formed a strong connection with George; he took him under his wing and played a positive role in not just his school life, but also his baseball life. Brother Mathias helped teach George how to hit, throw, and catch, and coached him to be an exquisite young baseball player. He also taught him how to run pigeon-toed. That pigeon-trot would become famous once George became older.

"I think a lot of Babe's good coordination came from when he lived at St. Mary's and played baseball with Brother Mathias," Julia Ruth Stevens, George's daughter, said. "He took a great interest in Daddy and Daddy loved Brother Mathias. He was the one that introduced Babe to baseball and showed him what the game was all about. Daddy did, he really did love Brother Mathias."[v]

Many kids who misbehave growing up turn their lives around through the influence of a positive person. For George, this was Brother Mathias. When his parents gave him up and left him shattered inside, Brother Mathias was there and was like a big brother or father figure to him. There may not be anyone who was as influential in George's life as Brother Mathias. He not only changed George's behavior for the better, but he also introduced him to baseball and helped him become good at it. In essence, he shaped George's life.

Brother Mathias worked with George every day and he was even able to get permission to spend extra time on the field helping George improve his skills. George could play any position but seemed to find his niche as a catcher. The challenge was that he had to play with a right-hander's glove even though he was a lefty. George made it work, though.

One boy who played with George said of his playing with a right-hander's glove, "He would catch the ball in the glove on his left hand, toss the ball straight up, drop the mitt on the ground, catch the ball again in his bare left hand and throw."[vi]

George's position changed, though, during a game where it was rumored he was taunting his own team's pitcher for not being able to get guys out and getting battered around. Brother Mathias decided to put George in as a reliever to show him that it was not easy to be a pitcher and to teach him a lesson. Well, or so he thought. Most of Brother Mathias's lessons were valuable, but this one backfired. It turned out to be easy for George. He pitched a stellar game, striking players out left and right. After that, George became a pitcher and he would stay one for a long time.[v]

Most importantly, George was a different person as he matured into his teenage years compared to when he was a wayward boy of seven. He had guidance. He had supervision. The correctional school had not only improved his behavior, but it also gave his life purpose. He found something he loved—baseball. He gained friends and had a mentor in life who taught him right from wrong. While his parents had given up on him, Brother Mathias did not. There was finally direction in his life and goals to work towards. George was no longer a problem child, but rather a problem for those who would go up against him in a baseball game.

George would never forget those days as a young child and his time at St. Mary's. It taught him a lot about life. As he grew up, he gained a special place in his heart for children who were left behind like he was. He could connect with them because he had been there himself. He knew what they were going through. A special empathy began to grow for those unfortunate children that would come back and play a much bigger role later in his life when he became famous and could give back.

Chapter 2: St. Mary's Baseball Career

Games became more serious at St. Mary's as George got older. It would be these games when he was a teenager that would hone his game as a ballplayer, eventually help spread the word about him, and attract more people by the end of his playing days there.

By 1912, George was beginning to make headlines in the local St. Mary's newspaper. The story one day was about how a 17-year-old player from that school put on a stellar performance crushing a double, a triple, and a home run in a game while also playing three different positions, including pitcher, where he faced six hitters and struck out all six. His legend was starting to grow.[vi]

Another time, the newspaper raved about how a player struck out 22 players in one game while also hitting .537. The walls at St. Mary's were apparently not high enough for Ruth, who kept blasting home run after home run out of the field.

Newspapers back in the early 1900s were not what they are now. Reporters could not attend games at St. Mary's and had to base their articles on word of mouth. Once, a rumor escalated about Ruth and it turned out they had the wrong Ruth. The "fake Ruth" was, in fact, a 24-year-old player from nearby St. Patrick's whose name was actually "Roth." Roth had hit nine home runs, far less than George. Stories in the paper were sometimes not entirely accurate, but one thing was certain: the real Ruth was pitching and hitting his way into the next stage of his life as he continued to outplay and outgrow his schoolmates. By his 18th birthday, he was already 6'2 and over 150 pounds.[vi]

Brother Mathias continued to work with George in all aspects of his game, improving his baserunning, his fielding, his hitting, and his pitching. He felt George was ready for the next big challenge as a player. The Brothers from St. Mary's set up a game with a neighboring college called Mount St. Joseph, a bit of a rivalry game between the two schools.

Mount St. Joseph's players were a bit older, definitely cockier, and more snobbish. They looked down on the St. Mary's boys, whom they generally perceived as juvenile troublemakers. Thus, they were excited for the opportunity to pile up the score on them and felt like they had the player to do just that—Bill Morrisette, their resident superstar. In 1913, Morrisette had thrown a no-hitter, one-hitter, three-hitter, and five-hitter against top college baseball teams. He was being recruited by the Orioles and was destined for success. He had a famous spitball that players could not seem to hit. He also was the team's star hitter on a team made up of many star-caliber hitters. The Brothers at St. Mary's arranged for George to start as a pitcher against them.[vi]

Just 10 days before the game, George went missing. Frightened about the game, he ran away. He did not want to play. School officials searched everywhere for him. Finally, a week before the game, the school's probation officer and night guard found him by the pier. George was severely scolded, disallowed from playing baseball for five days, and assigned hard labor as punishment. When he returned to the team, he had a heart-to-heart with Brother Mathias, who convinced him to play and pitch in the game despite his apprehension.

When the big day came, Morrisette and the Mount St. Joseph's team, feeling cocky and believing themselves better than the boys from St. Mary's, took the field ready to dominate their rivals. But George Ruth had different plans. He pitched a gem, reportedly striking out 14 players, including Morrisette. In fact, he ended up pitching a shutout. On the other end, the seemingly unhittable Morrisette was humbled by Ruth and his teammates. Ruth crushed Morrissette at the plate, who gave up a reported 6+ runs in the game.[vi]

Scouts were at the game to watch Morrisette, but by the end of the game, they wanted just one player: George Ruth. If you ever saw the movie *The Natural*, you would find parallels from that game to the beginning of the movie, with a bit of an ironic twist (which we will not spoil by saying too much for those who have not seen it yet). Just like that movie, the young star player who had all the hype surrounding him faced a young, left-handed pitcher that no had ever heard of in a one-on-one competition at a carnival. The unknown left-handed pitcher turned out to be the true talent at that carnival, getting the best of his star opponent. It was he whom the scouts turned their eyes to.

It was that game that helped propel George's career to the next level. Professional teams began to be interested in him. George would soon be leaving St. Mary's for the next chapter in his life.

Chapter 3: Minor League Career

Becoming "The Babe"

The Baltimore Orioles were the first team to become interested in George. The team was owned by Jack Dunn, a former major league player. At that time, the Orioles were a minor league team, not a major league one, so if George played with them, he would still need to be bought by someone else to make the majors.

Dunn knew baseball. He was a former player and managed the Orioles prior to owning the team. Dunn was also friends with Brother Gilbert from Mount St. Joseph's, who had told Dunn about Ruth's epic performances and invited him to watch Ruth's games.

Ruth was quite different than your typical ballplayer. While he was relaxed, calm, and poised on the field, he was also a boisterous, fun-loving guy who loved to talk and have fun. But at 18 years of age, George was not the same wild rule-breaker that he was at age seven. He knew right from wrong and was now responsible and grown up. Many of the Brothers thought very highly of him by this time. They would not have invited Dunn to come and watch if they did not feel he was responsible enough to live on his own and play professionally.

In February 1914, Dunn visited St. Mary's to watch Ruth and then give him a tryout. There, Dunn met the man who had mentored and trained George, Brother Mathias.

In the reported conversation between the two, Dunn explained his purpose for coming to St. Mary's. Brother Mathias simply responded, "Ruth can hit." When Dunn asked if he could pitch, too, Brother Mathias laughed and said, "He can do anything you want."[vi]

Tryouts usually take hours. Dunn needed only 30 minutes. After a few pitches and hits, he had seen enough. He wanted Ruth. However, because Ruth's legal guardians at the time were the Brothers at St.

Mary's, they had to grant permission to give him to Dunn, and then Dunn had to sign documentation to become his new legal guardian. Brother Mathias played a big role in convincing the school to release Ruth to Dunn, saying he had matured enough to make it on the outside. The Brothers agreed to turn him over to Dunn. Ruth was signed to a $600 contract with $100 guaranteed.

It was an emotional goodbye for George and the Brothers. They had taught him so much. They brought him up and gave him a home, teaching him how to act and how to play baseball. They had literally changed his life and paved a path for him to a brighter future. All the other boys and inmates stood outside and watched George leave. One boy was heard saying, "There goes our ball club."[vi]

Now on his own under the guardianship of Dunn, Ruth could visit other places. He decided to go to the saloon above his family home to visit his father and make amends with him. While a part of George was upset at his father for sending him to St. Mary's and not parenting him, he was also thankful for everything St. Mary's had done for him. He understood the pressure his father had been under and the circumstances that had led to his parent's decision to send him away. Sadly, his mother had already passed away in 1912, so George, Sr. was on his own. George, Sr. was happy to see him and offered George, Jr. a chance to help him out behind the bar, making a couple of extra dollars.

George, Jr. was mature now. Many young adults may hold grudges against their parents if they abandon them. But George, Jr. did not want to do that. He wanted to reconnect with his father even if he was not his legal guardian anymore. He would visit his dad on the weekends while he was in Baltimore playing with the rookies. He would then head to Florida for Spring Training, meaning it would be the first time in his life he would leave Baltimore.

When the time came for George to leave, he got on a train for the first time ever and headed for Florida to join the rest of the Orioles team. George was also on the train with other rookies who were going to Spring Training. One of those rookies that George connected with was none other than Bill Morrisette, the pitcher from Mount St. Joseph, who had also been signed by Dunn.

The train first stopped in Fayetteville, North Carolina, where George met the rest of the team. The first thing that struck George was their age. Most of these guys were well into their 20s or over 30. Baseball back then was a lot different than it is now. It is a kinder, much more welcoming environment for rookies playing today, but back in Ruth's day, rookies were treated harshly. They were given a hard time and were constantly hazed and ragged on. It was not easy. You had to have thick skin to be able to take it and deal with it. Plus, the fact that most of these Orioles players were much older than George made the hazing even tougher on him. George, however, had been through a lot as a young boy, so he definitely had the thick skin to take it.

The team stayed and practiced in Fayetteville before moving on to Florida. George did not know what to do with himself socially outside of baseball. Dunn was his legal guardian, so he would always stick with him wherever he went, following him around Fayetteville. The other players noticed this and hazed George for "following Daddy." They called George "one of Jack Dunn's babes."[v]

And thus, the nickname "Babe" was first introduced. And it stuck with him. After the hazing, players still called Ruth "Babe," not George.

Making an Impression

It did not take long for The Babe to make his presence known in the minor leagues. On March 7, 1914, Ruth made his debut at Cape Fear Fairgrounds in Fayetteville. In that first game, the team split up and played an intrasquad game, with the opposing team being called the Sparrows and George being on the team they called the Buzzards.[vii]

Ruth played shortstop and pitcher. When he came up to bat in the seventh inning, he was already 1-for-2 in the game. The first pitch he saw he launched incredibly deep into left field, leaving mouths agape around the field. It was the first of many home runs Ruth would hit as a professional ballplayer. The spectacular, 350-foot shot would forever be remembered, for it was the longest home run ever hit at that park. The Cape Fear Fairgrounds would later put a historic state marker there in 1951 to honor Ruth, and the newspaper article that reported the home run is now in a museum.[vii]

"I hit it as I hit all the others, by taking a good gander at the pitch as it came up to the plate, twisting my body into a backswing and hitting it as hard as I could swing," Ruth said.[vii]

George enjoyed his time spent in Fayetteville and was happily adapting to adulthood and loving life on his own. He was also experiencing many of the newer conveniences of the "modern" world for the very first time. He rode his first elevator at his first hotel and was mesmerized by it. One day, he did nothing but hit the up and down button, enjoying the ride. He also loved trains and was delighted every time he got on one. (Bear in mind, there were no airplanes back then—trains were how teams traveled from one city to the next.) Even if he did not ride on one, George would typically wake at 5 a.m. just to watch the train outside his place pass by.

Fayetteville, North Carolina has taken great pride over the years in that visit by Babe Ruth and the Orioles. They have their own separate Babe Ruth Day on March 7th each year. They also have a sign that proudly states, "The City Where Babe Ruth Got His Name."[vii]

The team played intrasquad games for a week. Dunn was watching and was extremely impressed by what he saw from Ruth. The Babe was striking guys out and constantly getting hits. *The Baltimore Sun* reported that Dunn thought Ruth was a superstar in the making.

"He's a whale with the willow...some of the drives he is making in practice would clear the right-field fence at Oriole Park," Dunn said in the newspaper article. "To my friend Brother Gilbert—Brother, this fellow Ruth is the greatest young ball player who ever reported to a training camp."[vi]

At Spring Training, the Orioles played games against anyone they could. Dunn arranged for the Orioles to play major league competition. Ruth was used mostly as a pitcher, not a hitter, at the time, which was where Dunn felt Ruth's talents were the most profound.

In their first series against the Phillies, Ruth pitched and struggled early on before settling down. As a reliever, he went through a stretch where he faced 29 hitters and gave up just 6 hits. Dunn moved Ruth into the starting rotation. Then against the A's, who were considered the best offense in baseball, Ruth gave up just two runs in helping the Orioles win, 6-2.

Dunn went back to Baltimore to hype up Ruth for when the team came back to play games there. The newspapers were all paying attention to what Ruth was doing. They were even calling him "Babe," not George. When they made their debut in Baltimore that season, Ruth took a beating, losing the game 12-5. But he was still making an impression.

The more Ruth played, the better he got and the more praise he received. Phillies coach Pat Moran said that Ruth "is a marvel for a kid just breaking in. I predict that within a few years Ruth will be one of the best southpaws in baseball." Oakland A's second baseman, Eddie Collins, added that "Ruth a sure corner. He has the speed and a sharp curve, and believe me, he is steady in the pinches."[vi]

Sometimes it is not about your performance, but how you carry yourself and how you learn from your tough experiences. This is what was impressing a lot of coaches and players. Even though Ruth would get roughed up from time to time, he was showing promise and poise. Any rookie is going to have rough moments. But the real pros know talent when they see it and Moran and Collins were just the first of many to comment on the burgeoning superstar's unflinching composure as they were witnessing it before their very eyes.

Dunn continued to schedule Spring Training games against the major league teams, bringing in a bigger audience to the stadium and getting his players more attention. Ruth was making the newspapers regularly as he took the mound and seemed to improve his pitching with every appearance.

In a Spring Training game against the Giants, a team that drew a huge crowd in Baltimore because of their superstar John "Mugsy" McGraw, the fans would leave with a new love for Ruth. With the Orioles leading the Giants 2-1 in the ninth, Ruth came in to replace the first baseman, who had lost his tooth. On the final play of a very tense game, Ruth received the throw from his fellow infielder for the third out. Ruth began to celebrate and wind up the crowd. He jumped up and down, threw the ball into the stands, and ran down the foul line encouraging the fans to cheer. The fans erupted in response to Ruth's joyful exuberance. Many would say, "Well, it was just a win in Spring Training." But for Ruth, it was more. It was the day he made an emotional connection with the fans, a day when the fans truly began to appreciate the personality that Ruth had to go with his growing talent.[vi]

The regular season started up with Ruth scheduled to pitch the second game of a series against the Buffalo Bison. It was a daunting start. First a walk. Then a wild pitch. Then an error on a pop fly. Then a hit-by-pitch. Before you knew it, Ruth had loaded the bases in the first inning of his first-ever, regular-season start. But Ruth was poised. He stayed calm and found a way to get out of the inning with no runs against him after a crucial strikeout to end the inning. From there, The Babe was in top form. He shut out the Bison and helped his team to a 6-0 victory in his first real game.[vi]

Ruth was pitching well enough to earn a contract raise from $600 to $1,200 for the season and then later to $1,800. It was still, however, an unusually low price for a league that was currently throwing around $10,000 and $20,000 to other 19-year-old players who did not seem much better than Ruth.

In July, Dunn began giving away Orioles players for fear of losing the team. He wanted to create capital to prevent the move, so players began to be sold. On July 8th and 9th, he sold two of his players for $23,000. The worry was Ruth was next. And, in fact, he was. On July 10th, Red Sox owner Joseph Lannin paid for the services of Ruth and two other players. Lannin paid Ruth $10,000 to come to Boston. While Ruth very nearly ended up with the Philadelphia Athletics, the Red Sox won the final bidding. Ruth was headed northeast to play major league ball for the Boston Red Sox.

Major League Debut and Return to the Minors

On July 11, 1914, Ruth made his first-ever major league start for the Boston Red Sox at Fenway Park. Ruth pitched a gem against the Cleveland Indians, whose lineup included Shoeless Joe Jackson. He held the Indians to one run in his first six innings before giving up two runs in the 7th, which tied the game at 3-3. But Boston rallied to take the lead and win, leading to Babe Ruth's first-ever major league win and complete game. Ruth started two more games but got battered around in one of them. He then sat on the bench for a month. He was 2-1 with a 3.91 E.R.A.

Ruth was also not making many friends with the team, many of whom did not like his brash manner and high-spirited behavior as much as the Baltimore players did. They felt he was a bit too extravagant for their franchise's high-brow image. The Red Sox were a recent World Series team and constant winners who had venerated talents such as star pitchers Joe Wood and Ray Collins on their roster. Both Wood and Collins chided Ruth behind his back for his exuberance, as neither player cared much for him. Yet, the fans *did* like him, which may have further fueled some of his teammates' resentment. Indeed, Ruth seemed to have a special connection with the fans wherever he went.

Thinking he needed some more work rather than just sitting on the bench, Ruth went back to the minor leagues to play for the Red Sox AA-team in the International League, the Providence Grays. In Ruth's first start for Providence, he hit two triples and pitched a complete game to help his team win, 5-4. In less than a month, Ruth piled up a 9-2 record and helped propel the Grays to the International League pennant.

George Ruth was also falling in love. He met 16-year-old Helen Woodford and married her in October that year after a whirlwind romance. He also received his driver's license, although he would soon get in a car accident while learning how to drive. After finishing his stint in the minors with a 23-8 record, it appeared as if Ruth was ready to head back to the big leagues permanently. He packed his bags for Boston for good.

It was quite the first year for the promising young star. Just a year ago, he was playing behind the walls of St. Mary's wondering if he would ever leave. Now he was on his own in Boston making a $3,500-per-year salary. He could come and go as he pleased in the offseason, and when he went to Baltimore to visit his home, he was treated as a local hero and celebrity. He was learning a lot about life. He was experimenting and his growing personality would soon put him in a positive light combined with some bumps along the way.

Chapter 4: Major League Career

The Red Sox (1915-1919)

Making the Red Sox roster would not be easy. The team had one of the deepest rosters of any team in Major League Baseball. Babe Ruth would need to have an incredible spring to make the cut and at first, it appeared that he would be the last man out. However, when pitcher Carl Mays went down in April with an ankle injury, Ruth got the call to head to Fenway Park.[vi]

As a pitcher, Ruth got off to a slow start with the team. He started off the year 1-4 and, if not for his bat, Ruth might have been sent back down to the minors. But Ruth was hitting to make up for his lackluster pitching. In his second game and playing the Yankees at the Polo Grounds, Ruth smashed a deep blast to right field, amazing the 5,000+ fans in attendance that afternoon. It was his first of 714 home runs as a Major League Baseball player. He had also shown some promise with his pitching, despite his record. By his sixth game, he began to settle in.

Ruth went 17-4 after his 1-4 start to finish his first year in the majors at 18-8. Throughout the year, his curveball was getting stronger and became even more unhittable as the season progressed. He finished with an impressive 2.44 E.R.A. over the course of 217 innings. As a hitter, Ruth got 92 at-bats and hit .315 with 4 home runs. Those 4 home runs were a lot, given that the league leaders back then rarely had over 10. Home runs were not a big thing in the early 1900s and whenever Ruth hit one, people were astounded at not just the evolution, but also how far he hit them. Ruth's four home runs led the team. He was sharp in his at-bats, although he only really hit on the days he pitched.

Ruth was the talk of Boston as a rookie and helped lead his team to the World Series that year against the Phillies. But Ruth was making a name for himself off the field as well, both in good and not-so-good ways. He had newfound freedom that he had never experienced before as an adult and he was taking advantage of it. He did not have enclosed walls around him as he had at St. Mary's. He did not have Jack Dunn anymore to guide him, either. Added to that were fame and money, and the overall combination of those things inevitably led to the temptations of a wild lifestyle for the young pitching phenom. After all, he grew up living in poverty and now had money to spend on whatever he desired. Ruth understandably wanted to take advantage of what life had to offer him outside of baseball.

Ruth's first year was the wildest, as one would expect. He lived life on the edge. He drove recklessly and ate hot dogs at every hot dog stand he could find. He even ate during games and had his fair share of drinks. While he started off drinking soda, as he got older, the soda would become beer. Ruth would often buy hot dogs during games and give them to kids in the stands while saving one for himself. His behavior as well as his appearance were more flamboyant than ever, as he always wore flashy suits when he went out and he used vulgar language around the clubhouse with the players.

Prior to the World Series, the Red Sox played a meaningless doubleheader in which Ruth pitched in what would be his final game of the season. Because of the way the rotation worked and the fact that the Red Sox had six starters, Ruth would not have the opportunity to pitch until Game 6 unless manager Bill Carrigan moved him up, which he did not plan to do. Therefore, during the World Series, Ruth spent most of the time on the bench, upset that he did not get a chance to pitch. He did get one at-bat as a pinch-hitter but he grounded out. Furthermore, Game 6 never came around since the Red Sox dominated the Phillies and won the World Series in five games. Ruth, a bit upset at his lack of participation but happy about the win, still celebrated his first World Championship. He also knew there were better days ahead.

After that season, Ruth went back to Baltimore to help his dad, who was struggling to keep his business going. Ruth, who had just received a $3,750 bonus for winning the World Series, used the money to buy the bar and keep his dad's business afloat. It would be that kind of generosity Ruth would exemplify over and over again in his life. Unfortunately, his father died tragically just three years later when he fell and hit his head while trying to break up a fight.[xix]

Prior to the 1916 season, Lannin was looking to cut his payroll. One of the stories exemplifying this was his proposed pay cut to outfielder Tris Speaker, a lifetime .322 hitter and outstanding outfielder, and Joe Wood, one of the Red Sox's star pitchers. The Red Sox were littered with talent and had some big, expensive contracts that did not mesh well with Lannin, who needed to lower their budget some. Speaker took offense to the pay cut and refused to re-sign, while Wood held out. Lannin sold Speaker to the Cleveland Indians for $50,000. Meanwhile, Wood did not play that season and would also join the Indians in the following season. With Speaker and Wood gone, fans were upset—but it was a chance for Ruth to become the new face of Boston.

He took advantage of his opportunity. That season was Babe Ruth's best as a pitcher. He finished 23-12 and led all of baseball with a 1.75 E.R.A. He also led the league with 40 games started and 9 shutouts. Of those 40 games started, he completed 23 of them. As a hitter, he was not as successful as the previous season, hitting .272 with three home runs. However, with the Red Sox struggling offensively that year without Speaker, they were able to get wins from Ruth, who helped the team grind out wins and make their way to another World Series. They would face the Brooklyn Robins and this time, Ruth would get a start and play a pivotal role.

The Red Sox were already up 1 game to 0 when Ruth started. Despite giving up an early run, he came up to the plate and tied the game with an RBI ground out.

After giving up his one run, Ruth pitched the next seven innings without giving up a single hit. The Robins could not touch him. Unfortunately, however, the Red Sox could not muster up any offense, either. The game went to the 14th inning and was in danger of being wiped out because of darkness. Back in those days, there were no lights. If a game was tied and got called off because of darkness, they would have to start it all over again the next day. It would have wiped out Ruth's performance.[vi] But luckily, that did not happen. The Red Sox found a way to get a game-winning hit in the bottom of the 14th to win the game and take a 2-0 lead on the Robins.

After the game, while in celebration, Ruth could be heard yelling at manager Carrigan, "I told you a year ago I could take care of those National League bums, and you never gave me the chance." Carrigan did not want to get into it and just said, "Forget about it, Babe."[vi]

In a nutshell, that quote defined who Ruth was. He was not afraid to speak his mind at all. He said what he thought. He was as outspoken a player as you would ever find, and honestly, it was a good thing. A lot of players today are fake and what you see is not always what you get. They hold back from speaking what they would like to say and instead say what others want to hear. That was not Ruth. If you upset him, he would let you know it. If he liked you, he would let you know that too. He was a joyful, happy guy but also had a bit of a temper and was never shy about showing that side of himself as well.

Just like the previous year, the Red Sox only needed five games to win yet another World Series. After the season, Carrigan left the Red Sox organization and changes were on the way. First, there was the Red Sox sale. Harry Frazee, an entertainment businessman, bought the Red Sox from Lannin. Frazee wanted a manager who was a player's coach, someone young who could add some fun to the team. He hired former second baseman Jack Barry, but that only lasted a season before Ed Barrow began managing the team in 1918.[vi]

There were also personal changes in Ruth's life. He began to settle down with his wife, Helen. They bought a new home with the raise he received, an 80-acre house with a farm that they dubbed "Home Plate Farm." He wanted to give Helen her dream home, something out in the open. She loved animals, and while Ruth was more of a city guy, he wanted to please his wife.[vi]

In 1917, several things happened. First, there was World War I, and several players around the major leagues, including with the Red Sox, left to serve in the war. Because Ruth was married, he was exempt from being drafted and so he continued to play ball. Ruth was also developing a new kind of confidence that helped with his play (but not with his behavior). As a pitcher, Ruth was still one of the best. He went

24-13 with a 2.01 E.R.A. and led the league with 35 complete games. That meant he finished 35 of 38 games started. Ruth also got some more at-bats and hit .325 while hitting two monster shots for home runs.[ii]

Ruth's behavior was not ideal, however. He got into arguments with umpires over balls and strikes. One time, he even hit an umpire who threatened to throw him out of the game. That incident got him fined and suspended. The suspension was supposed to last the entire season but Frazee was able to get it reduced based on the fact that Ruth brought in fans to the game.

The Red Sox were also not as successful that season. Duffy Lewis was called to the war that summer and not having him around affected the team. In the end, the Red Sox finished 90-62, second in the American League and out of World Series contention.

The 1918 season saw more changes for Ruth. Wanting to hit more and getting tired of pitching, Ruth asked the Red Sox during that season to switch him to a position player so he could hit. At first, the Red Sox were okay with it, but when they lost more players to the war, the Red Sox were thin at the mound and needed Ruth to pitch. Ruth boycotted and refused, sitting out in frustration. Manager Ed Barrow and Ruth got into a heated argument over it, but eventually, a compromise was reached where Ruth would hit but also pitch part-time. He got 317 at-bats that season and amazed the crowd with incredibly long home run shots, some of which left the ballpark. Ruth led all of baseball with 11 home runs that season and had a .300 batting average. Unfortunately, Ruth would always swing for the fence, so many times he struck out. He had 58 of them that season.[vi]

As a pitcher, Ruth started just 19 games. He went 13-7 with a 2.22 E.R.A. His efforts helped get the Red Sox back to the World Series, this time against the Chicago Cubs. Game 1 was all about The Babe. Barrow surprised everyone by starting Ruth in the opening game of the Series and Ruth delivered with his arm and bat. He pitched a gem, shutting out the Cubs 1-0. The one and only RBI came from The Babe himself who singled home a run in the fourth inning. Ruth was only used as a pinch-hitter for the rest of the series, which included a three-run triple in Game 4 which gave the Sox a 3-to-1 lead. He also pitched that game and shut out the Cubs in the first seven innings, making it 29 consecutive innings without giving up a run in a World Series, a record that would not be broken until 1961 by Whitey Ford.[vi]

The Red Sox won Game 6 to take yet another World Series, Ruth's third as a member of the team. Times were good for The Babe and Boston. Plus, the war was over and they would soon get the rest of their team back. Ruth continued to see a raise in his salary and was now so popular that he was overshadowing Ty Cobb as the talk of the league.

On the field in 1919, Ruth was still a powerhouse. He continued to be used more as a hitter and less as a pitcher. He only started 15 games that season and pitched well, going 9-5 with a 2.97 E.R.A. But it was his bat, not his arm, that was getting the attention. Ruth was blasting home runs out of every ballpark like no one in history had ever seen before. He led all of baseball in runs, RBIs, home runs, and slugging percentage.

Prior to 1919, the most home runs any player had hit in a season was 27 by Ned Williamson of the Chicago White Stockings in 1884. Ruth hit 29 bombs in 1919, breaking the record.[ix] He also became the first person in history to hit a home run in every city he visited. One home run against the Giants in an exhibition game was even rumored to go an astonishing 600 feet, although it was not confirmed.[vi] Still, people flooded to the ballpark to watch Ruth hit. The Red Sox were not even winning but people in Boston did not care. They just wanted to watch Ruth. Home run hits were much more of a rarity in the league back then, so it was stunning for the crowd to watch and they could not get enough of it.

Off the field, however, it was not one of Ruth's best seasons in terms of personal behavior. He continued to stay out late at night and have fun in the city, occasionally showing up to games hungover and angering Barrow. Ruth and Barrow often got into fights—sometimes fistfights—and it frequently landed Ruth on the bench. Ruth loved the Red Sox but he was growing increasingly frustrated with the team. Ruth was also having marital issues as his lifestyle contrasted with that of his laid-back wife, Helen. Rumors of affairs hit the papers and Ruth's late-night escapades understandably did not make her very happy.

Without Carl Mays, who was sold for $40,000, and without the presence of Ruth on the mound regularly, the pitching struggled and the Red Sox finished sixth that season in the American League. Most fans in other cities would be irate, but Boston had seen enough

World Championships. They now wanted to see Babe Ruth. He was the main attraction. His home runs mesmerized fans and kids came to the ballpark in droves simply because they loved to watch him hit. Ruth always gave them a show and made it a special point to greet the children during games.[vi]

Unfortunately for Boston owner Harry Frazee, however, fan adoration did not pay the bills unless it was accompanied by wins. The Red Sox were losing too much money and Frazee had to find a way to get out of debt. Little did anyone know at the time, but "The Curse of the Bambino" was about to strike Boston.

The Sale of the Century

This may be difficult to fathom, but the New York Yankees were not a particularly good baseball team before 1919. In fact, the same team that won 27 World Championships was once the laughing stock of baseball. Originally known as the New York

Highlanders, the Yankees had never made a World Series appearance, and from 1911 to 1918, they had just one winning season, which earned them a 4th place finish in the American League.

The team was owned by Jacob Ruppert and Tillinghast Huston, commonly known to others as "The Colonels." (In fact, they preferred to be called that in interactions.) Both owners wanted to draw in fans and win. They asked manager Miller Huggins what the team needed to do to get to the next level and compete for a championship. Huggins reportedly told them, "Get Ruth."[vi]

Huggins had heard rumors that Frazee was in financial trouble and The Colonels saw an opportunity to make something happen. When the discussions were initiated, the asking price seemed way too high, but Huggins insisted that Ruth was worth it, saying, "Bring him to the Polo Grounds and he'll hit 35 home runs at least."[vi]

Huggins went to Boston to try and negotiate the asking price down some. Frazee was asking for $125,000, which back then would be the biggest sale by far for any player. Discussions began and went on for a while.

Behind the scenes, there were also discussions between the Red Sox and Ruth. Ruth wanted a pay raise, who at the time, was making a lot less than Ty Cobb, the highest-paid player in baseball. Ruth was taking time to travel around the country "barnstorming" and considered not playing in 1919. However, he knew he could be traded and still wanted to play for Boston. He sent a telegram on Christmas to his personal secretary that he would play for Boston or not play at all.[x]

Both sides had their pros and cons. For Frazee, he needed the money, and selling Ruth would help eliminate his debts. He did not care so much for any players in return; he cared more about the money. On the downside, losing Ruth would destroy the team's future and anger Boston fans to no end. For the Yankees, bringing in Ruth would help their chances of winning a championship. It would be a blockbuster move that would excite the city and pack the seats. However, Ruth would not be cheap, no matter what the final asking price was. Plus, given the fact that they got most of their money from liquor sales and Prohibition would soon go into effect, they were concerned it might be too much for them to afford. They were also worried that the New York Giants, the city's other baseball team that played in the same stadium, would force them to build their own stadium should too many people go to games at the Polo Grounds. The Giants' owners owned the Polo Grounds. But in the end, the Yankees' owners realized it was simply foolish to pass up on Babe Ruth. If there was a chance to get him, they had to take that chance. The Colonels decided to pony up.

On December 26, 1919, Ruth was sold for $125,000 to the New York Yankees. Frazee got $25,000 upfront, along with four separate payments of $25,000 in the future. Frazee also received a mortgage loan of $300,000 to help pay for Fenway Park and keep the Red Sox there.[x]

For Ruth, the news came as a bit of a surprise. Huggins visited him and told him he had been traded. Ruth admitted that he knew there was a chance the Red Sox could deal him but did not think it would really happen. He was sad to leave Boston, but New York and the city life would be more for him. Huggins warned Ruth, however, that he needed to cut out the late-night partying and behave properly on the field in order to play for him. Helen was also not thrilled, as she enjoyed living on the farm and the city life was not for her. The move would only exacerbate the growing tension between the couple.

Ruth accepted the sale and said he would play hard for the Yankees. The fans in Boston, however, did not easily accept the loss of their beloved star. There was outrage and great displays of anger at Frazee. Newspapers called him out and fans booed him at games. Cartoons depicted Frazee in a bad light and attendance at the games plummeted. Fans and players pretty much threw up their hands and said, "There goes our team."

Frazee tried to defend himself, announcing that Ruth's off-the-field and on-the-field behavior was uncalled for and that he was the real reason for their poor 1919 season. He said Ruth "endangered the discipline of the whole squad."[vi] Fans did not buy it, however. They did not care about behavior. They cared about watching Ruth—he had thrilled them with his home runs and helped win them three MLB World Championships since 1915. Without Babe Ruth, they were in trouble. They wanted Ruth and they lost him to the Yankees.[vi]

So, the dubious deed was done, sending shockwaves throughout the league and fandom alike. The wheels of history—and perhaps fate—were turning. How would the trade impact the two cities? Historian John Thorn may have said it best: "If Boston was the cultural capital of 19th century America, New York City became the cultural capital of 20th century America when Babe Ruth arrived."[x]

Babe's Start with the Yankees (1920-1922)

When Babe Ruth arrived in New York, parties erupted. All of New York City was ecstatic that the Great Bambino was in their backyard. They thought a championship could now be theirs. Ruth's contract made him the highest-paid player in baseball, topping Ty Cobb. Players greeted him when he arrived and everyone wanted an autograph wherever he went. He was treated like royalty.

What made Ruth different than many players getting that kind of attention is not so much that he loved it (although he did), but that he especially enjoyed putting smiles on other people's faces. He was delighted to sign autographs because it made people happy. Many celebrities and athletes sign autographs today and smile for the cameras because they feel like they must for the sake of their image. Ruth was different. He loved being around people and making those encounters with fans special for them. During his time in New York, he would lavish his attention on fans even more, especially with the younger generation. Perhaps Ruth always remembered how awful it had felt to be neglected early in life and he wanted to make others feel the opposite.

The older Babe Ruth got, the more he also loved being around kids. In New York, this would become one of his trademarks. He was always giving when he could and trying to make them feel loved. No matter how bad things were at certain moments in his life, he always found time for them. When he arrived at the Polo Grounds before a game for the first time, he would always mingle with the kids. And as fans packed the stadium that season, Ruth delivered. There was no letdown. Ruth gave the fans of New York everything they wanted, and it made Boston feel even worse.

As for Ruth, his initial resistance to being traded to the Yankees quickly vanished as he was enthusiastically welcomed with open arms. One huge difference between New York and Boston were his teammates. In Boston when he first arrived, he was snubbed and players like Joe Wood acted harshly towards him. They mocked him a lot behind his back early in his career. He had had to let his bat do the talking to get them to quiet down. He loved Boston, but he did not have a good rapport with his teammates. In New York, it was not like that. He laughed a lot with his teammates and had fun. He went out with them more often than his teammates in Boston. It was a different feeling at Spring Training than what he experienced several years ago with the Red Sox. Benny Bengough, the Yankees' catcher, fondly called Ruth "Jidge" as kind of the New York slang version of "George," and it was a name that many Yankees ended up calling Ruth.[vi]

Off the field, Ruth did his best to behave. Frank Bodie, his good friend with the Yankees who would eventually not make the roster, was in charge of sticking by him at Spring Training in Florida and making sure he got from the train to the hotel room and back to the train in a timely manner. While Ruth still had his fun, he was more well-behaved than in Boston.

On the field, Ruth's first 12 games as a Yankee were a struggle. He dropped a fly ball in his first game in pinstripes and struck out three times in his second game. Then in Boston, his team was swept when Ruth unable to provide any offense. Following that, he pulled a muscle and had to miss some games. Other injuries popped up. He had no home runs in those first 12 games, while at the same time he had to watch his former team, the Red Sox, get off to a 10-2 start. It was there where the Babe turned it all around.

In a game against the Red Sox at the Polo Grounds, Ruth blasted his farthest home run yet in the MLB, going over the roof at The Polo Grounds, the first time any hitter had done that. From that moment on, The Babe made Frazee want to go into hiding. Ruth caught fire. Home run after home run. Hit after hit. Win after win. In May and June, Ruth broke a record with 12 home runs in one month. In a doubleheader on June 2nd, he hit three of them in Washington. By summer, there were over 38,000 adoring fans at The Polo Grounds to watch Ruth play. People were so packed in you could barely breathe. Prior to that season, the crowds were very sparse, kind of like you see at a Florida Marlins game in the middle of July. But now it was so overcrowded, the Polo Grounds and Giants management told the Yankees that they needed to get their own stadium, something The Colonels feared would happen if Ruth was successful. Luckily, they were able to find a location across from the Harlem River in the Bronx that would open in 1923.

Ruth kept getting better as the season progressed. He raised his average in June from .299 to .372. He hit .450 in June and had an incredible slugging percentage of .960, unheard of for a major leaguer. He continued to raise his average in July, getting it to .398, and broke his record from the previous month with 13 homers.[ii]

"Home runs executed by Babe Ruth are not mere home runs," W.O. McGeehan said, a writer for the *New York Herald-Tribune*. "Each home run seems to possess an individuality and eccentricities of its own. After the game, the multitudes linger in the lot to trace the path taken by the ball."[vi]

It cannot be said enough how Babe Ruth transformed the game. The home run was never a big thing in baseball before him. He rewrote the definition of the word and forever elevated its importance. Now, people looked at the game differently. He was the Home Run King. There was no denying it. What made it even more fun for Ruth is that he loved it. He loved hitting home runs because it thrilled and excited people. He loved giving them something to cheer for. One of Babe Ruth's best quotes is a simple one: "I like hitting home runs."[vi]

By the end of the season, Ruth led all of baseball in a long list of categories. He had hit 54 home runs, shattering his own record from a year ago. He led the league with 135 RBIs, 103 runs, 150 walks, and a slugging percentage of .847. Only three players topped Ruth's batting average of .376: George Sisler at .407, Ruth's former teammate Tris Speaker at .388, and Joe Jackson at .382. The Yankees finished 95-59, their best season in 10 years, and finished 3rd in the American League.[ii]

Ruth was a shining star in New York. Living on Broadway, he made acquaintances with many famous people. And though he was trying to behave in many ways those days, he still continued his reckless ways behind the wheel—and it nearly cost him his life. One time while traveling with his wife and coach, he was driving at a perilously high speed. Unfortunately, his car skidded out of control when trying to go around a curb, flipping over as his wife and Coach O'Leary were tossed from the vehicle. O'Leary nearly lost his life in the incident but eventually recovered, while Ruth and his wife were injured. Ruth hurt his knee and vowed to change his driving habits from then forward. Rumors swirled about the crash, with a newspaper headline in Philadelphia even declaring that Ruth was killed. Ruth, though, was still very much alive. And his powerhouse run with the New York Yankees was far from over.

The next two seasons Ruth continued to hit for power. In 1921, the Yankees won even more, finishing with a record 98 wins and winning the American League. They had a chance for their first-ever World Series that year and it was mostly because of Ruth. The Great Bambino was blasting home runs again at record levels. People were still amazed at what they were watching. Ruth hit 59 home runs! He broke his own record from a year ago and many of the shots were blasted right out of the ballpark. Owners began to look into adding higher walls or preventing people from parking behind the stadium, as some of Ruth's shots were actually hitting and damaging cars parked behind it. Ruth also added 44 doubles, 16 triples, 168 RBIs, 145 walks, a .378 batting average, and a league-leading .846 slugging percentage. His 177 runs were 32 more than the runner-up in that category.[ii]

In the 1921 World Series against the New York Giants, Ruth was battling injuries and had to play through games in a lot of pain. His body had taken a lot of wear-and-tear during the season. In Game 3, he cut his arm on a slide into third base. The cut was so bad that he had to be pulled from the game after already driving in two runs. In Game 4, with just one good arm, he blasted a home run over the fence in a losing effort.

The Babe's incredible home run stats did have a downside, however. Ruth struck out a lot. In 16 at-bats and 21 plate appearances in the Series, he got 5 hits but struck out 8 times. It was a common theme in his career. The man could hit, but he struck out a lot as well. It is common for home run hitters, though. Plus, given how banged up he was at that point, mustering up as much as offense as he did was impressive. The Yankees would lose the World Series to the Giants in six games, but it was not the last they would see of the Giants.[ii]

Ruth formed a partnership with Christy Walsh during 1921. Walsh, a writer and cartoonist, became the first-ever sports agent in professional baseball and would represent greats like Ruth, Ty Cobb, Walter Johnson, Dizzy Dean, and John McGraw. At the time, the role of entertainment media was evolving and began to play an important part in the lives of celebrities. Soon, most athletes, especially those of celebrity status, would need an agent.

Walsh played a huge role in Ruth's life, helping him with his image and setting him up with numerous radio and television stints during his career. A lot of the old film footage you see of Babe Ruth was set up by Walsh. Walsh's impact was huge because he promoted Ruth and helped spread the word at a time when baseball was hurting badly after the Black Sox World Series cheating scandal of 1919. Promoting Ruth brought people back to the stadiums, renewing their interest and their faith in baseball. Walsh also helped make Ruth more money with the Yankees and through advertising.

Prior to the 1922 season, Ruth wanted to showcase his skills off the field. He would do what was called *barnstorming*—going from city to city, playing in small, countryside fields and giving people a show, sometimes literally sleeping in barns. Baseball teams had done it since the 1860s so it was common and a way for players to make extra income in the offseason. It was a show for people who could not make it to major league games, and Ruth, someone who enjoyed making others happy, wanted to give those fans an opportunity to watch him play.

Unfortunately, the team owners spoiled the party and took action to bring barnstorming baseball shows to an end—they were not making any money from it, only the players were, and thus, they wanted to put a stop to it. The new baseball commissioner, Judge Kenesaw Landis, put legal grounds in place for players like Ruth not to do it. Landis was known as a tough judge, recently throwing eight White Sox members (nicknamed the "Black Sox" for their criminal behavior) out of the league for accepting money to lose the 1919 World Series.

Ruth, being who he was, was outspoken about his displeasure and rebelled. He refused to obey the new commissioner's outlawing of barnstorming. Fellow Yankee Bob Meusel and some other players also joined Ruth and went against the commissioner's wishes.

It became a battle of the two most powerful men in baseball, with Landis trying to show that the mighty Babe Ruth was not above the game. "This case resolves itself into a question of who is the biggest man in baseball, the Commissioner or the player who makes the most home runs," Landis said. While some said Ruth was doing it for the money, those who knew Ruth best knew that he was doing it more for the fans who did not get a chance to see him play. But as the whole drama came to a head, Ruth had to make a choice: either continue to barnstorm and never play Major League Baseball again, or accept the small penalty and go back to the Yankees.[vi]

Some owners were worried. Ruth was a major draw for Major League Baseball and at the time, the league was under attack in the wake of the Black Sox scandal, and not only that, but there was a new baseball league competing for the public's attention, the Federal League, which was looking to take advantage of the MLB's struggles to promote itself. If Ruth would have gone over to that league, it could have signaled the end of Major League Baseball. Ruth was so popular and beloved at the time that he could have conceivably even started his own league. The MLB needed Ruth.

In the end, though, Babe Ruth chose the Yankees. Landis withheld Ruth's World Series share and suspended him, Meusel, and several others until May 22nd for their disobedience. And just like that, the drama came to an end. The once hugely-popular practice of barnstorming would soon trickle to an end and become just another footnote in baseball history, although not immediately. Ruth would still defiantly participate in barnstorming shows occasionally in the years to come.

Ruth missed 46 games that season but still found a way to hit 35 home runs, which at that pace would have come close to his 59 home runs from a year ago if he had been able to play a full season. Once again, he had an impressive batting average, hitting .315 and a slugging percentage of .672.[ii]

The 1922 Major League Baseball Season was the worst for Ruth. His marriage with Helen was falling apart that year; she did not want to be around him in New York and went back to Massachusetts with Dorothy, their daughter. Ruth was also suspended and fined three different times, including once for getting into a fight with his manager.

Ruth continued to have moments that defined him—a polarizing figure. New York has always been known as a tough place that will boo you if you do not play well at any given time. Even Derek Jeter and Don

Mattingly received boos when they went into slumps. During one such time in an awful game at the plate, Ruth got his fair share of boos, and Ruth started to get angry. He threw dirt in an umpire's face after not liking his call, which promptly got him ejected. Then after he was ejected, he stormed into the stands to fight a heckling fan who was shouting obscenities at him. It was who he was—a loveable guy but a hothead who acted wildly and impulsively at times.[vi]

Ruth continued to battle umpires and face hostile fans where ever he went that season. It earned him a reputation for being temperamental that would stick with him for some time. Yet despite all the upheaval and drama of 1922, Ruth was still able to play a pivotal role in getting the Yankees to the World Series where they would once again face the Giants. However, hostilities lingered and distracted the team. Ruth charged the Giants' dugout after a player made personal attacks against him. Then Huggins got in a rift with owner Huston after a managerial decision that

Huston did not like. The Giants ended up besting the Yankees again and winning the World Series in an easy sweep.

It was Ruth's worst-ever World Series, hitting just .118 as he went just 2-for-17 without a home run. Fans continued to boo him at games. In fact, it was the only World Series he would ever play where a ball did not leave the park.[ii] That may say a lot about the season that had just passed, but it also hints that things were about to change once again for the better.

After that season, Ruth realized things had to change. He felt it was the low point of his career. He did not want to be a menace to New York. He told the fans that he would improve his behavior and put smiles back on the kids' faces. He went back to the farm that offseason with Helen, cut out drinking, and was looking to improve his life, which he did (although, unfortunately, illness overtook him for a brief time during that period also, an issue that would rear its ugly head in the future as well). Ruth began to work out more in the offseason to build his body back strong and lose weight. He had the help of a personal trainer and even dropped 13 pounds.

Meanwhile, prior to the 1923 season, the Yankees finished the completion of their new stadium. With the new-and-improved Ruth in residence, it would soon be bedecked with championship pennants.

The House that Ruth Built (1923-1928)

The Yankees purchased the new Yankees Stadium for $2.4 million and after construction in 1922, it was set to open. The stadium was huge and could fit up to 62,000 people, although The Colonels were somewhat disappointed because they originally thought it would seat more. They would try and find ways to get more people to fit in because they needed it with Ruth.

The Yankees were poised to get better. They signed an up-and-coming young star from Columbia University named Lou Gehrig, who would end up actually making

The Babe even better, as the two would have a bit of a friendly competition with each other in future years that only added to their success.

Also prior to the season, Ruth was reaching new lows in his relationship with his wife, Helen. Despite multiple attempts to reconcile and find common ground over the years, the two continued to live separate lives. They were just too different, with Ruth's flamboyant, city lifestyle and Helen's quiet, country preferences. The two would eventually separate down the road just as Babe was falling in love with someone else: Claire Hodgson, an actress with whom he shared more similar qualities and really hit it off with. She had also been previously married and had a daughter named Julia. Claire's presence in New York would help Babe, as not only did he fall in love, but he also finally and truly settled down.

The Yankees' first game in the new Yankees Stadium was one that Babe Ruth would never forget. On April

18, 1923, it seemed only fitting that the Yankees played none other than his old team, the Boston Red Sox. The announced attendance of 74,117 was the biggest crowd yet for a Major League Baseball game. The huge, triple-deck ballpark was jam-packed and the air was buzzing with excitement. In the third inning, Ruth came up to the plate and blasted the first home run out of the new stadium. The crowd roared as Ruth trotted around the bases—his trademark, pigeon-toed trot, of course—as he waved and cheered along with the fans.[xviii]

Writing his column that night after the game, Fred Lieb wrote about Ruth's ability to draw, excite, and entertain a crowd. He called Yankees Stadium, "The House that Ruth Built." Little did Lieb know, that moniker would stick in the heads of sports fans everywhere for generations. It lasted for the entire 85 years of the ballpark's existence, until it was finally taken down and a new stadium was built in 2009, a stadium that some now call "The House that Jeter Built."[xviii]

"I think that was the proudest moment of his life, and I think he believed that it would never have been 'The House that Ruth Built' if he had not hit that home run that day," Claire Hodgson said. "He definitely talked about it more than any other home run he ever hit, including his 60th, which, after all, only broke his own record of 59."[xvii]

One of the best quotes about that iconic moment comes from former Yankee pitcher Bob Shawkey, who pitched that opening day game. He said the atmosphere around Ruth was insane.

"Once the Babe homered, the fans cheered forever," Shawkey said. "Can you imagine anyone paying any attention to me that day? Babe owned the day. And that was just fine; he was born to be in the spotlight. It was his day from beginning to end."[xvii]

That was Ruth. No one entertained and drew an audience in more than the Sultan of Swat. Sure, people came to see Gehrig and Mantle and Jeter and DiMaggio as time went on, but it was never quite the same. Ruth brought baseball to New York. Before him, the pastime did not exist there. The fans barely showed up. Babe Ruth changed all that. Many baseball historians agree that Opening Day in 1923 could not have been scripted any better for the Yankees. And what made it even more deliciously satisfying was the fact that the game was against the Red Sox and marked the beginning of the "Curse of the Bambino."

"There was something about the man that he'd always rise to the occasion and make the fans happy," Marty Appel, a baseball author and historian and a former Yankees public relations director, said about Ruth. "He did not disappoint anyone when he homered on Opening Day '23 and just put his seal on this being a game of monumental significance."[xviii]

The Yankees 1923 season was one of their best ever. They were dominating all of the MLB. Attendance was somewhat down outside of New York because other teams realized they did not have a chance and could not match what Ruth and the Yankees were doing. The Yankees were separating themselves from the rest of the American League and ended up winning it by 15 games over the Tigers. The Yankees finished with a record of 98-54, their best record yet, while the Red Sox fell victim to the Curse of the Bambino. They finished a horrendous 61-91 that season, 37 games back. Fenway Park had awful attendance, its worst yet.[vi]

For the first time in a long time, Ruth was having fun on the field. Ruth, Bob Meusel, Wally Pipp, and Whitey Witt helped lead the Yankees offense while Lou Gehrig was brought up late in the season and hit .423 in 13 games. Sad Sam Jones led the pitching staff with 21 wins. That season, Ruth led baseball in seven different categories. Incredibly, his .393 batting average was not one of them as Harry Hellmann hit .403. But Ruth hit 41 home runs that season, crossed home plate 151 times, and drove in 130 runs, all of which led the league.[ii]

Whatever hostilities the fans had in New York before that season were immediately forgotten. What boos? The Babe was New York and New York was The Babe. He had made his amends and they cheered every hit and home run that season with unquenchable enthusiasm. The city was buzzing. One again, the Yankees had to face the formidable Giants in the World Series. But this time, they were determined to come out on top.

Despite losing Game 1 because of an inside-the-park home run by Casey Stengel, marking the eighth straight World Series game the Giants had beaten the Yankees, the Bronx Bombers bounced back. Babe Ruth smashed two home runs in Game 2, one of which went clear over the roof at The Polo Grounds where the Giants played and helped lead the Yankees to a 4-2 win. After Stengel shut the Yankees out in Game 3, the Yankees offense returned again with a vengeance. They won the next three games 8-4, 8-1, and 6-1 to win their first-ever of 27 World Championships.

Ruth had made up for his poor World Series showing the following season, hitting .368, belting three home runs, and scoring eight runs. He not only won his first championship as a Yankee, but he was also named the Most Valuable Player of the 1923 season.[ii]

Riding the high of a championship season, Babe continued to barnstorm, despite the commissioner's wishes against it. He did it for the kids. He wanted to go to places where the kids were and greeted them as he got off the train He loved talking to them. One time after a tour, 6,000 kids swarmed Ruth on the field. He was joyous and conversed with all of them, even throwing the baseball around with a few of them.[v]

Just before 1924, Ruth came down with a nasty flu (a too-common ailment for him) that caused him to shed some of the 240 pounds that he had been carrying at that time. The Yankees did not play as well that season, although they still won an impressive 89 games, good for second in the American League. But Washington was three wins better after overtaking the Yankees with a 16-5 stretch at the end of the season, keeping Babe and the Yanks out of the World Series. Part of the reason for the Yankees' slight setback was that they had lost one of their star pitchers, Carl Mays, to the Reds.[ii]

That year, Ruth had a great experience when he got to meet President Warren Harding before a game. Most athletes would say something like, "It is an honor to meet you" or "I'm so thrilled" when they first meet the President. What did The Babe say? He just wiped his head with a handkerchief filled with sweat and greeted the President with, "Hot as hell, ain't it, Prez?"[vi]

Once again, Babe just said what was on his mind and did not censor himself because of who he was talking to. Ruth was not one to get into politics. He just treated the President like everyone else. He was gracious, but he was also The Babe.

Ruth's health began to noticeably decline as he repeatedly fell ill with colds and the flu during 1924 and 1925, although he also still persisted in putting up impressive numbers. He continued to drink, eat, and gain weight. However, every time he seemed to put on weight, he seemed to lose it just as quickly because of illness. In Spring Training in 1925, Ruth had a temperature of 106. That said, he still played, still hit for average, and still pounded out home runs.

During a train ride in Washington, D.C. Ruth collapsed and had to be taken to the hospital. Ruth was taken by a stretcher into St. Vincent's hospital in New York City. While people speculated about how serious it was, doctors said it was just a bad case of the flu and that he would be fine. Ruth's wife Helen, who was still with him at that time despite their faltering marriage, was there by his side and going through a tough time herself—Helen would eventually check herself in for a nervous breakdown.

Once Babe got back into action, he began a friendship with the great Lou Gehrig. Gehrig spent most of 1923 and 1924 in the minors and was only occasionally brought up during the season to get some MLB experience. Management was so impressed by what they were seeing, however, that they activated him to the roster in 1925 where he would begin to steal some of the headlines away from Ruth. The Babe loved the attention, so when Gehrig started to lure some of it away, Ruth, who was a bit jealous at first, did only one thing: he tried to be better. Gehrig, feeling equally competitive, tried to do the same. As a result of the rivalry, Ruth and Gehrig put on a show in 1925 and the years to come that eventually developed into an incredible friendship.

Gehrig and Ruth had a great bond. The two had a deep respect for each other and loved the competitive challenges of trying to best the other. Over time, the two gelled and it helped define the Yankees for part of the 1920s. Ruth would describe Gehrig as like a little brother to him.[xi]

The two also shared a very common similarity. Both were born from mostly German parents. Ruth even spoke German in his earliest years. Ruth, who was abandoned by his German parents, visited Gehrig's home regularly, ate dinner with them, and spoke German with them. Their relationship did hit a bump later on (more on this later), but they reconciled and will always be linked.

In 1925, Gehrig hit 20 home runs while Ruth hit 25. Ruth was sick and missed a lot of the season, only playing in 90 games. The next year would be a much better one, though.

In 1926, Ruth got back to his powerful ways although he still battled illness that cost him some time. Gehrig and Ruth combined for 262 RBIs in 1926, with Ruth leading all of baseball with 153 of them. Ruth also belted 47 home runs while posting a .372 batting average and a .737 slugging percentage. He helped get the Yankees back to the World Series, an epic seven-game series against the Cardinals. Ruth belted four home runs that Series and batted .300. Gehrig also had a great series, hitting .348. In Game 7, Ruth hit a home run to tie the game, but the Cardinals got the final say with a great pitching performance from Jesse Haines to win that game 3-2. The Yankees would be back, though.[ii]

Then came 1927, maybe the most famous Yankees team and season ever. They were so good they earned the nickname "Murderer's Row." Much of the attention focused on Ruth and Gehrig, as the two men went back and forth with home runs in an epic showdown. It was the home run battle for the ages.

The competition between the two intensified that year over who would hit the most home runs. Ruth had the record at 59 and was always seen as the Home Run King, but Gehrig was the new guy starting to steal the spotlight away and it looked early on in the year as if he might break it. When headlines started to speculate at the possibility, Ruth wanted to protect his record and some may say that he "got a little fuel in his belly." Ruth wanted to be the best and the competition only made the team better.

When August rolled around, Gehrig was leading Ruth in home runs and had fans flooding into the stadium to see the two in action and get a glimpse of the competition. Just then, Ruth's fire burned more than ever. He not only started hitting home runs at a more rampant pace, he was destroying the ball. He hit 17 home runs that month and finally passed his fellow star when Gehrig cooled off a bit. With four games left, Ruth stood at 56 home runs for the season, three behind his own record. He wanted to break it. First, he hit a grand slam. 57 homers. The next night, two more left the ballpark. That was 58 and 59. He tied his record but wanted one more. On Sept. 30th, the final game of the season, Ruth crushed a pitch off pitcher Tom Zachary, his 60th home run of the season, and a new record.[vi]

As a whole, the Yankees offense was amazing. Ruth and the Yankees seemed to separate themselves from opponents in the middle of the game, so much so that it was called "Five-o-clock Lightning." The Yankees broke an all-time record that year and it still stands as one of the top-five seasons in history. They won 110 games, losing just 44. They won their league by 19 games. Murderer's Row, indeed. Ruth hit .356, Gehrig .373, Tony Lazzeri .309, Bob Meusel .337, and Earle Combs .356.

In the World Series that year, the Pittsburgh Pirates had no chance against the Yankees lineup. It was an easy sweep. The Pirates were competitive in two of the games, but the Yankees dominated them. Ruth went 6-for-15 and knocked out two balls for home runs. He and Gehrig combined for 11 of the team's 19 RBIs in that Series.

The rivalry between Ruth and Gehrig got a bit heated during the home run showdown. While the two mostly had a great friendship prior to 1927 and later on in their lives, there was a rough patch in the middle that emerged during the 1927 season. The two had different lifestyles and the home run competition served to add some tension. Ruth loved to drink and smoke cigars while Gehrig smoked pipes and was more of an educated, Ivy League man. Ruth liked to mingle with the poor while Gehrig liked to hang out with the rich. Gehrig was also stealing a lot of the attention, winning the Most Valuable Player Award in 1927 over Ruth.[xi]

The following season, not much changed. Once again, the Yankees were the best team in baseball, winning 101 games. Ruth's power continued as he hit 54 home runs while teammate Gehrig blasted an additional 32. The team as a whole was just as good as the season before, until the end when injuries took their toll and they finished the season in a slump. Gehrig was banged up, Mark Koenig and Lazzeri were hurting, and the St. Louis Cardinals were going into the World Series on fire.[vi]

The Yankees may have limped into the World Series, but they were far from willing to roll over for the Cards. Despite their slump at the end of the regular season, the Yankees offense was too much for St. Louis to handle. They dominated in all four games, outscoring the Cardinals 27-10 and sweeping them.

That was eight straight World Series wins for the Yankees. Ruth and Gehrig led the way again, accounting for more than half of the team's RBI's that series. Gehrig topped Ruth by one more home run, hitting four of them.[ii]

Ruth's Connection with Kids

"At Mobile, there was a large crowd. After the game the teams went to their hotel and had dinner and Ruth still had not come back [from the game]. He finally came in about eight o'clock without his cap; his shirt was torn, his fielding glove was tied to his belt with a cord, and his baseball suit was all muddy with Alabama clay up above his knees. The reporters asked Ruth, 'Where were you?' Ruth replied, 'There were about 75 kids who stayed in the park and wanted to play ball. I spent all the time since the game hitting flies and shagging flies with the kids.'"[vi]
– Joe Conlan, former Major League player and umpire

Ruth and children were like a magnet to each other. They went where he went and he went where they went. He did not just love talking with them and driving them around, he would play baseball with them, too, even coaching them. If Babe was not a big-league player, he would have probably made a great Little League coach.

In a way, Babe Ruth was a big kid himself. He felt like part of his carefree youth was taken away when he was given up by his parents at such an early age, so him acting like a big kid and enjoying himself in his 20s was just him trying to get back the fun that he missed early in his life.

"Babe was unusually good with kids," Ruth's teammate, Bill Werber, said. "You know, when he would leave Yankee Stadium—he was an immaculate dresser—and the kids would walk all over to him and he would just continue to stand there and sign autographs for them until he was told he had to leave. He would go to hospitals to see sick kids that asked to see him and he would not bring a photographer or a reporter with him."[xii]

Ruth proved time and time again that he did not do it for the attention. He did not care about reporters seeing the private moments he had with the children. That was personal to him. It meant a lot. The hospital turned out to be a place that Ruth loved to visit. Unfortunately, there were times he visited it as a patient, but the times he loved most was when he went as a visitor, brightening up the sick children's spirits.

One of the best stories about Ruth and kids came in 1926 during the World Series. Johnny Sylvester was 11 years old and a huge Yankees fan. He listened to every game and idolized Babe Ruth. One day, Sylvester got in a horseback-riding accident and was bedridden at his house with a very serious bone infection that doctors said could cost him his life.[xiii]

The Yankees got word of Sylvester's fandom and illness and several of the players signed a ball for him. Ruth signed the ball and wrote a note on there, promising Johnny he would hit a home run for him at Wednesday's game, which happened to be Game 4 of the World Series. That game would mean a lot to Ruth.

He delivered on his promise and hit a home run. But Ruth was not done. He hit another…and then another. Three home runs.[xiii]

A week later, after the World Series was over, Ruth personally went to Sylvester's home and paid Johnny a visit in Essex Falls, New Jersey. Ruth also invited Johnny to Yankees Stadium the following season and promised he would help win the team a pennant in 1927. Johnny could not have been happier and was inspired by Ruth's visit. Somehow, he began to miraculously improve. Johnny visited Babe that next season at the Stadium, then went on to Yale and even served in the Navy during World War II. Recently, when Sylvester was tracked down and asked by a writer if the story was true, Sylvester showed the writer the baseball which read "I'll knock a homer for you on Wednesday. Babe Ruth."[xiii]

Ruth also met with Leon Fichman, a childhood actor who starred with Ruth in a few short films. "He was the nicest man I ever met," Fichman said. "He was so nice to all of us kids when we worked together for those two weeks. I'll never forget a minute of it. I remember sitting on his lap and he put his arms around me and made out that ball for me that said, 'To Leon, from one left-hander to another, Babe Ruth.' I'll never forget it. One of the most important days of my life."[xii]

Many children shared similar stories. In 1931, Ruth visited 300 children in a hospital and was dressed as Santa Claus. He gave out presents to them, something he would do regularly during Christmastime. In 1933, six orphans in Passaic, New Jersey were able to stop a train that was about to go into a deep ditch and cause a major accident that would have killed people. Ruth heard about what those boys did and visited them at their orphanage. He called them heroes. He talked with them, signed baseballs, and even played a little baseball with the boys. A few years later, he commented in an interview on what those kids did.[xiv]

"Remember those kids in the Passaic orphan asylum over in New Jersey a few years ago?" Ruth said. "It was a real act of quick-thinking heroism. Without question, they saved lives. Remember what Johnny Murdock and his pals said that night when the railroad officials told them they could have almost anything they wanted as a reward? They said, 'We don't want any reward. But could you please let Babe Ruth know what we did?'" Ruth said he was touched by this and wanted to show his appreciation.[xiv]

Ruth appreciated the youth. He inspired them. After a game, he would pick them up and talk to them. Ruth would say whenever he was going through a tough time in his life, he could always count on the young children to make him feel better. So many pictures over the years have been shared by adults who shared their pictures of them as a child with Babe Ruth. He was perhaps the most inspirational figure to the younger generation that ever lived.

The Twilight of Ruth's Career (1929-1935)

By 1929, Babe Ruth was now entering the last stage of his career. After being in the majors for 15 years, he had already accomplished so much. He had won six World Series titles. He broke the home run record and then broke his own record three more times. He had a lifetime batting average of close to .360 and had won a Most Valuable Player Award. He led the league in runs eight times and RBIs five times. He was even once known as the best pitcher in baseball before he became a hitter. (Ruth did actually pitch in games as a Yankee a few times spanning his first year with the team, 1920, and 1921. However, after that, Ruth became a full-time hitter.) The most important of his accomplishments, however, was how he helped popularize baseball in New York and brought a city—and a sport—to life.

Things began to change in Ruth's life in 1929. First, his wife Helen died tragically. Helen had gone through a lot during those last few years and had become distant with Ruth but still kept in touch. The two had remained married, albeit separated. She died in a fire in her home in Watertown, Massachusetts. Ruth wept very much at her funeral service.

Later that year after mourning his wife's death, he moved on and married Claire. They had been together for years while Ruth was separated from Helen. The two had settled down and Ruth became a father figure to not just his own daughter, Dorothy, but also to Claire's daughter. Claire helped change Ruth for the better, taking care of him when he was sick and trying to protect him when he did something dangerous. She also helped him to limit drinking. Many said she was a very positive influence in his life.[vi]

Ruth, now 34 years old, could still hit. In 1929, he led the league again with 46 home runs and hit .345. Many said he was looking calmer out there. Gehrig also contributed to the offense, hitting 35 homers. Despite Ruth, Gehrig, and Lazzeri helping lead the offense, the pitching was a different story. The Yankees struggled from the mound. Despite leading the league in offense, they were in the middle of the pack in pitching. They also lost their manager, Miller Huggins, who died in September from *pyemia*, a common sepsis disease that was frequently life-threatening before the age of antibiotics.

The Yankees finished with 88 wins and in second place behind The Philadelphia A's, who had become the new hot team in baseball led by Jimmie Foxx and Jimmy Dykes. The A's would go on to win the 1929 and 1930 World Championships.

Ruth was slowly beginning to slow down once 1930 rolled around. He used to play full seasons but now was taking days off. His home run numbers stayed high in 1930 and 1931, hitting 49 and 46 home runs respectively, as was his hitting numbers, but he did not have the same speed he used to have, nor the same energy as when he was in his prime. In a game on

Opening Day in 1931, Ruth collapsed from pain in his leg, hospitalizing him for 10 days.

The team was still winning games, finishing second in 1930 and 1931, including a 100-win season in 1931, but the Athletics at that time were still beating them out in the pennant. The Yankees were still led by Ruth and Gehrig offensively, and Lefty Gomez was a young rookie who had given the Yankees' pitching staff their strength back. But Foxx and the A's were just better at that time.

Huggins' death started to lead Babe to consider managing. Ruth offered to coach the Yankees. However, the team's general manager then was none other than Ed Barrow, who was once with Ruth when he was in Boston and he had a rocky relationship with him. Barrow rejected the idea and instead hired Bob Shawkey and then later, Joe McCarthy.

Baseball, as a whole, was struggling. The Great Depression was in full force and many stands around the league were thin. Ruth's continued presence, however, kept the game alive. People still filled the stands when he played. He gave people something to come to the ballpark for. He was still hitting home runs, even when the MLB tried to de-juice the baseball to stop home runs from going out so many times. It did not stop Ruth.

When 1932 came around, Ruth was dealing with all sorts of injuries. His body had taken a beating over the years, between the injuries, the flu, the stomach problems, and everything else. Baseball was becoming hard. Ruth, also an avid golfer, had to quit playing because his leg pain was so bad. Ruth was in so much pain, he would hit and then be removed from the game in the latter stages for a pinch-runner. He would hobble over to the bench. Still, Ruth led the Yankees' offensive onslaught that year. They scored 1,002 runs, the most in baseball, and Ruth hit an impressive .341 while slugging 41 home runs. For one of the few seasons in his career, however, someone hit more home runs than him. Jimmie Foxx hit 58, the third-most ever in a season. Gehrig also broke a record by hitting four home runs in one game.[vi]

The Yankees found themselves back in the World Series that year against the Chicago Cubs. It was that Series that brought about one of the most famous baseball moments in all of history, one that is still talked about today. The Yankees had already won Games 1 and 2 in Yankees Stadium and traveled to a wild and frenzied Wrigley Field in Chicago. The atmosphere could be described as nothing more than chaotic. The fans were not kind to Babe and were razzing him to no end at batting practice. Ruth could be heard shouting, "I'd play for half my salary if I could hit in this dump all the time." The fans responded by throwing lemons at him. The old Ruth would have probably charged the crowd, but now he just tossed the lemons back at them.[vi]

During batting practice, the fans also got on Gehrig. Ruth told Gehrig, "Let's put on a show for them." And they did. Ruth and Gehrig traded home run after home run in practice, only leading to more anger from the fans.[vi]

In the top of the fifth inning, the game was tied and had a lot of suspense and tension to it. The two dugouts were trading insults at each other and the crowd was only making things crazier. Ruth came up to the plate and got the worst abuse yet. Players from the Cubs dugout and the fans were shouting obscenities at him and booing him ferociously. More lemons were thrown on the field. They only called him more names after the first strike was called. Ruth held up one finger. "That's one." After a couple of balls, a second strike went past him. The two dugouts continued to bark at each other, and one Cubs player even came out to harass Ruth.[vi]

Ruth was cool and calm. He then waved his bat and right hand at the dugout and then pointed two fingers. Where they were pointing, well, that has been a question people have been trying to answer for almost 100 years now. Fans in the stands have said it was at the fence to indicate he was going to hit one over it on the next pitch, but others, like Cubs catcher Gabby Hartnett, have said he was pointing his fingers at the dugout indicating, "That's two strikes."

After that point, the place went into an even bigger ruckus at what was happening and what Ruth was doing. A riot was on the verge of breaking out. Pitcher Charlie Root tried to put a curveball past The Babe for strike three but instead, a loud crack was heard. The place watched in awe as Ruth smashed the pitch and hit a ball deep into the centerfield stands, the longest home run ever at Wrigley Field.[vi]

It became known as "The Called Shot." The debate will always go on about whether or not he actually called it or was merely pointing to the dugout, but whatever the case, it has always been perceived as a called shot, even after a raw video from the moment came out. We can say this much, however: Lou Gehrig came up to bat after Ruth and followed with a home run of his own. Furthermore, Gehrig seemed certain of what Ruth did. "Did you see what that big monkey did? He said he'd hit a homer, and he did." The crowd, which was harassing Ruth just a couple of minutes ago, had all of a sudden grown quiet. The Yankees went on to win that game. Years later, audio of Ruth was also produced in which he could be heard saying after the game, "I told him I was going to hit the next pitched ball right into centerfield for a home run."[vi]

"That's the first time I ever got the players and the fans going at the same time," Ruth also said after the game. "I never had so much fun in my whole life."[vi]

That was what baseball was for him—fun. He loved it. He enjoyed it. It was not so much about the records or the money. For Babe, it was more about enjoying life, including the competition and all the smack talk that came with it. Some people hate when fans attack them and get into it. Babe was the opposite. He relished it. When fans and players got into it, Ruth just gave his famous laugh and savored it even more.

The next day, the Yankees sealed the deal and won their fourth World Championship by beating the Cubs again. Ruth once again had a great World Series in what would be his last. Over his career, he played 41 postseason games and finished with 15 World Series home runs, a record that would last until 1964 when Mickey Mantle passed him, eventually hitting 18 home runs in the World Series. He also hit .333 in the World Series and drove in 33 runs.[ii]

Ruth's age and the wear-and-tear to his body continued after that World Series. His home run numbers in 1933 and 1934 continued to come down and in 1934, his string of eight straight seasons hitting over .300 ended. The face of the game shifted to Gehrig and Foxx. The Yankees continued to win in those seasons, finishing second each year. Ruth did make the first-ever All-Star Game in 1933, a game that would become a huge event as time went on. In fact, Ruth hit the first-ever home run in an All-Star Game, which was held at Comiskey Park. He also added a single and helped the American League All-Stars to a 4-2 win. If an MVP award would have been given then, it would have gone to Ruth, but Major League Baseball did not start giving out All-Star Game MVPs until 1962.[ii]

Ruth had thought of retiring after the 1933 season, but he wanted to accomplish hitting 700 home runs. He was still 14 shy of the mark after 1933. He also really wanted to become a manager. On July 13, 1934, facing the Tigers, Ruth blasted a ball 480 feet over the fence at Tigers Stadium for the 700th home run of his career, a landmark that would last for almost 50 years until Hank Aaron hit that many.[vi]

Ruth was disappointed and let down after the 1933 season, however, when he thought he was to become the next manager of the Yankees. McCarthy's contract had run out and he was led to believe he would be next in line. He really wanted the position. However, McCarthy re-signed with the team and remained the team's manager, upsetting Ruth.

There were rumors that other teams had offered Ruth the chance to manage their teams, but Ruth wanted to stay in New York and one day manage the Yankees. Then came the Tigers. Their owner wanted to trade for Ruth and let him become their new player-manager of the team in 1933. Barrow tried to convince Ruth to accept the trade, but Ruth instead chose to go on vacation first and said he would consider it when he came back. By the time he did come back, the Tigers had moved on and signed catcher Mickey Cochrane, who won World Series with the team later that decade.[vi]

By 1934, Ruth was just a memory in New York. Lou Gehrig hit for the Triple Crown, something Ruth never was able to accomplish. He did not make the All-Star Game that season. His numbers were down, and as is the tradition in New York, if you do not perform, you get booed. He felt it was about time to hang it up. He still had great moments that 1934 season. Boston honored him and packed Fenway for the 20th anniversary of him debuting with the team. They gave him a standing ovation when he came up to the plate. You do not see that very often for a Yankee at Fenway. The Babe tipped his cap back to the fans.[vi]

Ruth still wanted to play but he told sportswriters that he would not play again for the Yankees unless he would manage. In the end, however, Barrow struck a deal with the Boston Braves, a contract which stated that Ruth would be assistant manager and vice president for the team and play whenever he wanted. The agreement led Ruth to believe that he would become manager one day of the team. But he was duped. He learned the next season that the deal was not what he thought it was and he had been fooled into thinking he would become a future manager of the team in an effort to bring in more fans to a struggling fan base. This led to a very cold relationship between Ruth and the owner, Emil Fuchs.

Ruth did indeed bring in huge crowds in Boston, but his play was anything but stellar. He was 40 then and hobbling around. Ruth did not have the power or the youthful vigor of his prime anymore. He played just part-time with the Braves, realizing he was not helping the team much at the plate. In 72 at-bats, he struck out 24 times in 1935. He hit only six home runs. Once Ruth realized he would not become manager one day for the Braves, he was upset. He got in fights with Fuchs and decided it was time to retire. On May 12th, he asked the Braves organization to put him on a voluntary retired list, meaning he would stay on the roster and part of Braves property while retired. He also thought it could keep his managerial hopes alive.

However, that meant he could not play for 60 days and the organization refused.

On May 25, 1935, Ruth was at the bottom of the barrel. Hitting in the .100s and his legs about to give out, Ruth faced the Pirates at Forbes Field. Forbes Field was a tough park to hit home runs in as it had a high right-field roof. In the first inning, Ruth smashed a home run over the wall and into the right-field stands. In the third inning, Ruth came up again and belted another shot into the upper deck. In the fifth, he hit a single. He was 3-for-3. Then in the seventh and facing Guy Bush, Ruth connected on a curveball and hit a monster shot that left Forbes Field. It was the longest home run there ever. It was Ruth's 714th⎯and the final home run of his career. The fans cheered. He tipped his cap as he hobbled around the bases.[vi]

Ruth tried to continue to play while others urged him to retire. He wanted to hold up his end of the bargain with the Braves, but his anger towards Fuchs got worse and it got to the point where Ruth wanted nothing to do with him. He asked again to be put on the voluntary retired list, meaning he could not play for at least 60 games. After that, Ruth never came back. He left the game. He still wanted to manage, but never got a chance.

"It was the biggest disappointment of his life—no question about it," Julia Ruth Stevens said. "He felt even if he did not make good—and he was sure that he would—he should have been given the chance. That's what hurt him the most."[vi]

Not every life is perfect. Even the greatest people of our time have dreams they do not always get to achieve. Ruth had a great career, maybe the best of any ballplayer ever, and had so many great qualities about him, but that was his biggest disappointment: not making it to manager. He wanted to be one so badly but it never happened. Perhaps if he had remained healthy later on in his life, it could have happened, but illness overtook him much to soon and began to end his life.

Still, Ruth's career will go down as one of the greatest ever. He was a star pitcher and hitter that single-handedly brought both Boston and New York to life. While he may not have gone out exactly the way he wanted, he still went out a champion, beloved by a nation, and the best player of his generation. Many say that he is still the best.

Chapter 5: Personal Life

Early in Babe Ruth's baseball career, he found ways to occupy his time outside of the game. Most of his off-seasons were spent barnstorming when he took trains around the country, showcasing his talents to those in the Midwest and the West who could not see baseball games in person. The Babe loved to travel and enjoyed playing for kids and viewing all the different parts of the country. He loved the scenery and the contrast between the East and the West. There was even a short video out, *Play Ball with Babe Ruth*, where Ruth gets off a train and sees a bunch of young kids playing baseball and he goes out to play with them. Ruth did a lot of little videos like that with kids.[xv]

Ruth's love life was a bit tumultuous early on, before he finally settled down. He met his first wife, Helen, in 1914 when she was a 16-year-old waitress at a luncheonette. But one of Ruth's mistakes is one that many young people make: he got married too early.

Ruth never truly fell in love before, so the first girl he met that he liked, he wanted to marry. He would learn with time that love needs to develop before you take the next step.

While Babe enjoyed the city, he also enjoyed his time on the farm with Helen where they lived. It was an escape for Ruth away from the craziness of urban life, although eventually the city life would envelop him and he could not get enough of it. He was very young and enjoying some of the many temptations that fame and money could sometimes bring, which undoubtedly added considerable strain to his marriage and inevitably led to the couple's separation.

Babe Ruth was a good and kindhearted man, but he was also flawed, like so many of us, and far from innocent. In 1921, Babe and Helen adopted a child, Dorothy. Years later, it was revealed that Dorothy was actually Ruth's own natural child, who was conceived from one of Ruth's mistresses. Later, Ruth also became a father figure to Julia, who was the daughter of Claire Hodgson.[vi]

Yes, Ruth was a flirt, just like many ballplayers when they are young, and somewhat of a womanizer. However, you also have to understand that Ruth did not have a life like most high schoolers. He was locked in at St. Mary's—a school strictly for boys. So, when he got this new freedom followed by fame, it was hard not to be sucked in. Ruth and Helen shared too many contrasts that became more and more apparent as they both matured. It eventually pulled the two apart. Helen headed back to the farm in Massachusetts to live while Ruth played in New York City all season and then traveled in the offseason. While they stayed married, the two struggled to get along a lot of the time and drifted apart, living separately for most of their marriage.

When Ruth met Claire, it was different. She understood Ruth better because she had lived that high-profile, city life herself. She helped him when he was down in ways Helen could not. She lived in the city with Babe and was there by his side during his illnesses after baseball. Claire was a model and a showgirl who had appeared in movies. She, like George, enjoyed parties but had a strong head on her shoulders that helped Babe considerably as he got older. She had a huge affection for him and it was easy to see why Babe was so close to her.[xv]

George was also very religious. As a devout Catholic, George did not want to divorce Helen. He stayed married to her until she passed and he avoided moving too fast with Claire because of it. He regularly attended church services and donated to the church.

Baseball with no Babe Ruth felt strange, but Ruth found a life outside of it. He struggled at times when the game tried to bring him back, but when he was not around it, he became your ordinary, retired family man. He got back to playing golf once he regained his strength in his legs, something he also loved very much. The Babe was a phenomenal golfer, shooting in the 70s, and even thought he could possibly play with the pros one day.

Ruth also spent his days as a devoted father, watching his children grow up and being there for them whenever they needed him. He walked his daughters down the aisle when they got married and was a loving husband to his second wife, Claire.

"Daddy (Babe) and Mother (Claire) loved entertaining people at their home," Julia Stevens Ruth said. "Daddy loved his home and all the things that went on—all the holidays. They would almost always have a New Year's party and I can remember some of the various people that used to come—Hoagy Carmichael would come and play the piano. That was just fabulous.[xvi]

"He liked to have people around him but there were lots of evenings though where we would play cards or play checkers with Momma and he would always beat her and she would get mad and walk out! He was so grateful to have an honest to goodness family, due to losing his mother at such a young age."[xvi]

Ruth's daughter really helped illustrate the type of man he was, especially as a father and a husband to Claire. Growing up, he did not have a family. He made up for lost time and enjoyed his life outside of baseball. He made the best of it. More importantly, he had a huge heart. He was the typical big, loveable guy you always wanted to be around.

The Giving Babe

Ruth's personal story illustrates the life of a ballplayer with newfound freedom, but it also reveals how special he was. While he had his wild moments as a notoriously reckless driver and a partier, he had his soft side, too. Ruth genuinely cared for people, especially children. He gave back in tremendous and touching ways. As a player and a man of means, he frequently visited hospitals and orphanages and donated to sick and unprivileged children as much as he could. After retirement, he did even more, especially during World War II. Ruth was a huge supporter of the troops.

Ruth once teamed up with his old rival, Ty Cobb, in 1941, and played a best-of-three golf match in Boston with money going to war charities. Ruth also worked with the Red Cross and helped raise $100,000 after Pearl Harbor and frequently volunteered his time to do what he could to help the troops in the war.

In 1943, Babe Ruth and Mel Ott also held a fundraiser where they raised money in a hitting contest with war bonds being donated for each hit. Ruth also went to hospitals at least four or five times a week, visiting families, whether they were impacted by the war, or were just ill and needed someone to give them encouragement. Ruth's goal in life was to cheer up spirits. It was to make others feel good when they were down. He did not want sad faces and it hurt him inside when he saw kids sick. He did whatever he could to inspire them.

Ruth returned to visit Yankees Stadium a few more times for charity functions to help raise money for the war. In 1942, he and Walter Johnson faced off in "The Duel" in-between doubleheaders. Johnson, the former Washington legendary pitcher, faced Ruth, who ended up knocking out two home runs into the Yankees' bleachers.

Before he passed, Babe also established The Babe Ruth Foundation, a charity that gives money to children who are sick and in need. When Ruth passed, a lot of his money went to the Foundation and to children in need. Today, the foundation still exists and gives money to children in hospitals.[xii]

Staying in Baseball

In 1938, a few years following his retirement, Ruth got the offer to get back into baseball when the Dodgers gave him a $15,000 contract to be their first-base coach. Ruth was excited, as it was his chance to maybe get a managerial job down the line, although it was not likely to be with the Dodgers, who already had Leo Durocher lined up to take over as manager. While Ruth coached first base, his main job was to draw fans in Brooklyn who showed up just to see Ruth. For the most part, he was nothing more than a gate-attraction.

Ruth pondered coming back into baseball as a player while first base coach and there was talk about it, but at age 43, the game had passed him by. He tried hitting in batting practice but the magic was just not there. Then Durocher got in a fight with Ruth when reporters were giving Ruth credit for a hit-and-run call that helped lead the Dodgers to a win. The two scuffled and management was not happy. They told Ruth they would not renew him for the following season.[vi]

The word spread about the incident, and with Ruth's prior fights and well-known temperament already on owners' minds, he sadly never got another chance to manage or play in baseball.

In 1939, Ruth learned of Lou Gehrig's disease and visited the Stadium on "Lou Gehrig Day" to hear his former friend and sometime-foe give a speech that not just brought Gehrig to tears, but also Ruth. Gehrig had played for 2,130 straight games up until 1938, a record that would last until Cal Ripken, Jr. broke the streak in 1995. Gehrig pulled himself from the lineup after not feeling well in 1938 and never played again. After Gehrig's speech, Ruth went over to him and went to shake his hand. A couple of seconds later, the handshake turned into a hug and an embrace. Whatever wounds there were between the two were buried that day. For the first time all day, Gehrig smiled. It was a trademark of Ruth; he knew how to put a smile on someone's face. Ruth wept when Gehrig died two years later in 1941.[vi]

Ruth's health began to deteriorate in the summer of 1946. His eye was in terrible pain. The whole left side of his face was swollen and he could not eat. His eye was shut. Doctors did not know what was wrong but Ruth was bedridden in the hospital for a month. Finally, a malignant tumor was found around the major artery in his throat. He was diagnosed with throat cancer. Surgeons operated and were able to remove part of the tumor, but not all of it. Ruth was dying.[xvi]

Ruth lost weight and was losing his hair from the cancer. But just when he was feeling down, he got a lot of love and support. He received thousands of letters from fans and thousands more from kids, wishing him well and a fast recovery. It brought Ruth to tears.

Ruth was released from the hospital and then paid one last visit to Yankees Stadium on "Babe Ruth Day" on April 27, 1947. In Babe Ruth's speech, he talked about how much baseball meant to him and that it was the only game that mattered.[xvi]

"You've got to let it grow up with you, and if you're successful and you try hard enough, you're bound to come out on top, just like these boys have come to the top now."[vi]

Fans gave Ruth a standing ovation after he tipped his cap and gave them a wink. Ruth's daughter described Ruth as very emotional after that speech, and he was in a lot of pain as he gave it. But he continued to try and entertain others, even as he slowly succumbed to his own terminal illness. He traveled one day to the hospital and played Santa Claus for young children with polio. He visited orphanages and greeted young kids. He continued to give back to the community as much as he could.

Babe Ruth died on Aug. 15, 1948, but his legend will never be forgotten. The Great Bambino is remembered just as much today as he was in his prime.

Chapter 6: Ruth's Legacy

In 1936, Babe Ruth was inducted into the Baseball Hall of Fame, one of the five first-ever players to make it into Cooperstown. But his legacy goes far beyond just the Hall of Fame.

Ruth will be remembered for so much more than his batting and larger-than-life personality. His unusual swing produced a .342 lifetime average along with 714 career home runs. Babe kept his feet very close together at the plate and actually resembled Joe Jackson, who Ruth once called "The greatest hitter I ever saw." Ruth and Jackson both set a standard for hitting in which, as lefties, they put a lot of weight on the left rear foot. Keeping their feet close together, they aimed their right shoulder at the pitcher. What resulted was a propeller-like swing with lots of power. It could result in a spectacular home run, but it led to a lot of strikeouts as well, too, because of the science of the swing.[vi]

"Throughout his career of twenty years, Ruth never changed the basics of that gorgeous, gargantuan arc—a swing that fascinated the crowd as much as the personality of the man behind it," wrote legendary sportswriter Grantland Rice. "To watch Ruth go down swinging, often sprawling from the violence of his cut, was almost as exciting as seeing him blast one out of the park."[vi]

Ruth led the league in strikeouts five times during his career. Of course, he also led the league in home runs 12 times. He made the home run what it was.

Simply put, Ruth changed the game. He revolutionized it. Baseball was not anything like it was before Ruth. Baseball never used to have the full stands it did before Ruth's time. It was just a game that two teams played, but Babe Ruth helped make it one of the greatest pastimes of generations to come. He brought popularity to the game not only in the cities of Boston and New York but around the world.

His 714 home runs stand third all-time, but those 714 arguably meant more because of when he did it. When Ruth played his first game as a major leaguer, Roger Connor held the record for most home runs with 138. Ruth passed Connor's record by 1921. When Ruth hit his 700th home run, Lou Gehrig was the next closest at the time at 348, and Jimmie Foxx would ultimately become the next closest to Ruth for a long time when he ended his career with 534 homers.

Over time, Willie Mays, Mickie Mantle, and Hank Aaron came along and challenged Ruth's numbers, but only Aaron passed him. Barry Bonds would pass Aaron, although speculation has risen about how many of those home runs he would have hit without the use of performance-enhancing drugs.[ix]

Ruth was also seen as the saving grace of a game that was dying after the Black Sox scandal of the 1919 World Series fix. That scandal put a black mark on the game that many thought was done forever. But Ruth revitalized it and made people forget about what had happened. He restored the world's trust, sparked a level of electrifying excitement never seen before, and made it okay to once again enjoy and love the great game of baseball.

What if there was no Babe Ruth? The game may have died in the 1920s. Lou Gehrig was the next great player to come along, but he said he was inspired growing up by watching Ruth. Who knew if Gehrig would have been so great without The Babe, or Jimmie Foxx, or the many others that followed. Ty Cobb was a great player, but he never revolutionized the game like Ruth. He never brought new fans and captured the hearts of the younger generation the way that The Babe did.

So many stories about Ruth are still talked about today, some 100 years after he played. The "Called Shot" and whether it was really called or not is a fun debate people continue to have at dinner parties and in baseball parks to this day. If any baseball fan had the chance to go back in time to witness any moment in history, that 1932 Cubs-Yankees game would be near the top of the list. Then, there are the many stories about Ruth's special bond with kids—stories about how Ruth helped inspire Johnny Sylvester and other young children by hitting home runs for them and making them feel happy. Stories about how Ruth was the personification of the American dream, a rags-to-riches guy, growing up poor, given away by his parents, and then becoming one of baseball's greatest players. Stories about his friendship and feud with Lou Gehrig and their ultimate home run showdown that makes the McGwire-Sosa showdown seem like nothing.

Babe Ruth was also famously known as the catalyst who triggered bad luck for the Boston Red Sox for generations. It was "The Curse of the Bambino." Boston had won five World Series before 1919, three of them with Ruth. After they sold Ruth to the

Yankees, a sale that resulted in some of the worst outpourings of anger from Boston fans towards an owner, the Red Sox did not even make the postseason again until 1946. In fact, during Ruth's time with the Yankees, the Red Sox finished dead last in the American League nine times! It took until 2004 before the Red Sox finally broke the curse and won a World Series, a postseason where they came back from 3 games to 0 down against the Yankees, ironically. During that "curse" period, the Yankees had already piled up 26 world championships.

In the current history books, Ruth stands first in all-time slugging percentage (.690), third in all-time home runs (714), second in all-time RBIs (2,214), fourth in runs scored (2,174), third in total walks (2,062), and second in on-base percentage (.474). Before the steroid era came, Ruth stood second all-time in single-season home runs, passed only by Yankee Roger Maris, who hit 61 in 1961. Since then, he has been passed by Bonds once, McGwire twice, and Sosa three times.

And, oh yeah, let us not forget Babe was a pitcher, too. He stands 17th all-time in career E.R.A. at 2.77.[ii]

There are so many lessons that we can learn from the legacy of Babe Ruth. First, the importance of generosity and giving. Making others happy should be one of our top priorities in life—and just because you achieve success and fame, does not mean that ends. In fact, for Ruth, achieving financial security helped him because he could help others more often. Another lesson, to enjoy and live life to its fullest. Ruth did just that. Every second of his life was meaningful. He was outspoken, indulgent, and did what he wanted more often than not, although sometimes that got him into trouble. He always made the time to appreciate everything that life had to offer, from the grandest opportunities to the most mundane.

And the most important lesson of all—*anyone* can make something out of their life, no matter how bad it starts out. George Herman Ruth began life as a juvenile delinquent. He was given away and finally came out of St. Mary's with no money, only a new outlook on life and hope. He worked his way to a better life through hitting home runs and embracing the game he loved as his chosen career. In the process, he changed the game forever. From nothing, Babe Ruth became more than something.

Babe Ruth never took his success for granted. He knew he was lucky to be taken in as a child and mentored by Brother Mathias at St. Mary's, and he never forgot that. He never forgot the boys of St. Mary's, or the many lessons he learned there. He went on to become one of the greatest success stories the world has ever witnessed. And in many ways, he devoted his life to paying it forward. Yes, they were hard and humble beginnings, but it shaped who he was and who he ultimately became.

Conclusion

If you go to Yankees Stadium and visit Monument Park, there you will see Babe Ruth's granite plaque. On it, it reads "George Herman 'Babe' Ruth. 18895-1948. A Great Ball Player. A Great Man. A Great American."

Over time, multiple documentaries and movies have been made about Babe Ruth, one of very few ballplayers to have such an honor. Perhaps only Ruth, Jackie Robinson, Lou Gehrig, Roger Maris, Ty Cobb, and Mickey Mantle have been able to say they have had movies made about them. The topic of Ruth, as well as the ghost of Ruth, even appears in the movie *The Sandlot*, when a young boy tries to recover a baseball bearing Babe Ruth's signature out of the backyard where a huge English Mastiff has it collected.

They also made the movie "The Babe" in 1992 which is, well, fiction in so many ways, and you'll see what is meant by that if you watch it. They portray Ruth as a fat kid, which he was not. He was lean and muscular most of his playing days. They portray his father as just doing away with him and never seeing him again, which also is not true. Ruth often saw his father, especially after leaving St. Mary's. The movie also over-exaggerated the "partying" side of him. Ruth did have his fun, but not to the extent that the movie portrays. And those are just a few of the movies discrepancies. The whole movie is a myth with a few accuracies mixed in here and there.

In the debate about who is the greatest player of all time, there really is no right answer. We all have our favorites and our reasons. Some may say Babe Ruth while others argue for Robinson or Mantle or DiMaggio or recent greats like Jeter, Griffey, Trout, or Nolan Ryan. But Ruth, and perhaps Jackie Robinson, will go down as the two men who forever changed baseball and the argument can be made that Ruth changed it more. If Robinson did not come along, another black player eventually would have to bring about the changes that he did. But in the case of Babe Ruth, had he not come along the game itself may not have survived. The game was hurting badly and losing fans, and without The Babe breathing new life into it, it very well could have died. So we can argue that Babe Ruth changed the game of baseball perhaps more than anyone else in history.

His legend will go on and never die. The laugh he had. The smile and the wink. The controversy he loved to stir up. His outspoken nature. His quest for fun. His erratic behavior. His big heart and giving nature. There are not enough words and adjectives to describe him, and while he also had his shortcomings, as we all do, the positives far outweighed the negatives.

Babe Ruth is a hero, a symbol of triumph over diversity, and an enduring icon to multiple generations. The greatest baseball players of today idolized him and wanted to be just like him when they grew up. And nowadays, people *still* want to be like the legendary

Babe Ruth—and the more people we have like that today, the better the game is and forever shall be.

Final Word/About the Author

I was born and raised in Norwalk, Connecticut. Growing up, I could often be found spending many nights watching basketball, soccer, and football matches with my father in the family living room. I love sports and everything that sports can embody. I believe that sports are one of the most genuine forms of competition, heart, and determination. I write my works to learn more about influential athletes in the hopes that from my writing, you the reader can walk away inspired to put in an equal if not greater amount of hard work and perseverance to pursue your goals. If you enjoyed *Babe Ruth: The Inspiring Story of One of Baseball's Greatest Legends,* please leave a review! Also, you can read more of my works on *David Ortiz, Mike Trout, Bryce Harper, Jackie Robinson, Aaron Judge, Odell Beckham Jr., Bill Belichick, Serena Williams, Rafael Nadal, Roger Federer, Novak Djokovic, Richard Sherman, Andrew Luck, Rob Gronkowski, Brett Favre, Calvin Johnson, Drew*

Brees, J.J. Watt, Colin Kaepernick, Aaron Rodgers, Peyton Manning, Tom Brady, Russell Wilson, Odell Beckham Jr., Bill Belichick, Charles Barkley, Trae Young, Gregg Popovich, Pat Riley, John Wooden, Steve Kerr, Brad Stevens, Red Auerbach, Doc Rivers, Erik Spoelstra, Michael Jordan, LeBron James, Kyrie Irving, Klay Thompson, Stephen Curry, Kevin Durant, Russell Westbrook, Anthony Davis, Chris Paul, Blake Griffin, Kobe Bryant, Joakim Noah, Scottie Pippen, Carmelo Anthony, Kevin Love, Grant Hill, Tracy McGrady, Vince Carter, Patrick Ewing, Karl Malone, Tony Parker, Allen Iverson, Hakeem Olajuwon, Reggie Miller, Michael Carter-Williams, John Wall, James Harden, Tim Duncan, Steve Nash, Draymond Green, Kawhi Leonard, Dwyane Wade, Ray Allen, Pau Gasol, Dirk Nowitzki, Jimmy Butler, Paul Pierce, Manu Ginobili, Pete Maravich, Larry Bird, Kyle Lowry, Jason Kidd, David Robinson, LaMarcus Aldridge, Derrick Rose, Paul George, Kevin Garnett, Chris Paul, Marc Gasol, Yao Ming, Al Horford, Amar'e

Stoudemire, DeMar DeRozan, Isaiah Thomas, Kemba Walker, Chris Bosh, Andre Drummond, JJ Redick, DeMarcus Cousins, Wilt Chamberlain, Bradley Beal, Rudy Gobert, Aaron Gordon, Kristaps Porzingis, Nikola Vucevic, Andre Iguodala, Devin Booker, John Stockton, Jeremy Lin, Chris Paul, Pascal Siakam, Jayson Tatum, Gordon Hayward, Nikola Jokic, Bill Russell, Victor Oladipo, Luka Doncic, Ben Simmons, Shaquille O'Neal, Joel Embiid, Donovan Mitchell, Damian Lillard and *Giannis Antetokounmpo* in the Kindle Store. If you love basketball, check out my website at claytongeoffreys.com to join my exclusive list where I let you know about my latest books and give you lots of goodies.

Like what you read? Please leave a review!

I write because I love sharing the stories of influential athletes like Babe Ruth with fantastic readers like you. My readers inspire me to write more so please do not hesitate to let me know what you thought by leaving a review! If you love books on life, basketball, or productivity, check out my website at claytongeoffreys.com to join my exclusive list where I let you know about my latest books. Aside from being the first to hear about my latest releases, you can also download a free copy of *33 Life Lessons: Success Principles, Career Advice & Habits of Successful People*. See you there!

Clayton

References

i. "23 Babe Ruth Nicknames and the Story Behind Them." *FindNicknames*.com. Nd. Web.

ii. "Babe Ruth Career Stats." Baseball-Reference. Nd. Web.

iii. "Babe Ruth Biography." Biography.com. 27 Apr 2017. Nd. Web.

iv. "Ruth's Illness and Passing – The Nation Mourns." *Babe Ruth Central*. Nd. Web.

v. "Ruth's Childhood." *Babe Ruth Central*. Nd. Web.

vi. Adomites, Paul and Wisnia, Saul. "Babe Ruth Enters St. Mary's Industrial School for Boys." *HowStuffWorks*. Nd. Web.

vii. Sandler, Roberta. "Babe Ruth's First Flight in Fayetteville." *The Baltimore* Sun. 27 Feb 2014. Web.

viii. Apple, Charles. "The Bambino: A Tribute to Babe Ruth." *The Spokesman Review*. Nd. Web.

ix. "Yearly League Leaders and Records for Home Runs." ball-RefeBaserence. Nd. Web.

x. Leavy, Jane. "Why on Earth Did Boston Sell Babe Ruth to the Yankees?" *The New York Times*. 30 Dec 2019. Web.

xi. Goldman, Steven. "75 Years Later, Babe Ruth's Hug Means Almost as Much as Lou Gehrig's Speech." *SB Nation*. 8 Jul 2014. Web.

xii. "Babe Ruth's Effect on Children." *Babe Ruth Central*. Nd. Web.

xiii. "Livicari, Gary. "The Heart-Warming Story of Babe Ruth and Little Johnny Sylvester. *BaseballHistoryComesAlive.com*. 23 Jan 2016.

xiv. Cowen, Richard. "The Day Babe Ruth Came to Passaic to Honor Six Orphans who Changed the Life of Others." *NorthNewJersey.com*. 3 May 2018. Web.

xv. "Wife's Death Opened Secrets of Personal Life of Babe Ruth." *Retro Simba*. 7 Jan 2019. Web.

xvi. "Babe Ruth, Family Man." *Babe Ruth Central*. Nd. Web

xvii. "Babe Ruth's Legacy." *Babe Ruth Central*. Nd. Web

xviii. Rieber, Anthony. "The Day That Ruth Built the House That Ruth Built. *Newsday*. 26 Mar 2020. Web.

xix. Kaltenbach, Chris. "Rare Photo of a Young Babe Ruth and his Dad Up for Auction." *The Baltimore Sun*. 24 Apr 2018. Web.